ESSEX COUNTY, VIRGINIA

DEED and WILL ABSTRACTS

1699-1701

Ruth and Sam Sparacio

The Antient Press Collection
from

Colonial Roots
Millsboro, Delaware
2016

Colonial Roots
Helping You Grow Your Family Tree

ISBN 978-1-68034-341-0

Originally printed 1991 by The Antient Press
Printed in the United States of America

ESSEX COUNTY, VIRGINIA
DEEDS & WILLS
1699-1701

p. 1 William the Third by the grace of God King of England, Scotland, France & Ireland, Defender of the faith &c. to JNO: CATLETT, WM. MOSELEY, THOMAS EDMONDSON, EDWARD THOMAS, FRANCIS TALIAFERRO, BERNARD GAINES, ROBERT BROOKE, JNO: BATTAILE, JNO: TALIAFERRO, JAMES BOUGHAN, FRAN: GOULDMAN, RICHD. COVINGTON, DANL. DOBYNS & ROBT. PAYNE Gentlemen Greeting.

Know yee that we have assigned you & every one of you joyntly & severally our Justices to keep the peace in ye County of Essex & to keep & casue to be kept all Ordinances, Statutes of our Kingdom of England & Laws of this our Ancient & Great Colony & Dominion of Virga: made for ye good of ye Peace and for ye conservacion of ye land for ye quiet Rule & Governmt. of ye people in all & every of ye Artickles thereof in ye sd County according to ye force form & effect of ye same do chastise punish all persons offending agt: ye forms of these Ordinances Statutes of our Kingdom of England, Laws of this our Colony or Dominion, or any of them in ye County aforesd., to cause to come before you or any of you all the persons who shall threaten any of our Leige People either in their bodyes or burning their houses to find sufficient security for ye peace or for ye good behaviour of ye people, And if they shall refuse to find such security, then to cause them to be kept safe in Prison untill they find such security, Wee here also assigne you or any of you JNO: CATLETT, WM. MOSELEY, THOMAS EDMUNDSON, EDWARD THOMAS, FRANCIS TALIAFERRO & BERNARD GAINES shall be one to meet at ye usual places of holding Courts in ye County of Essex aforesd. at certaine dayes according to Law to hear & determine all such contionsions & debates betweene party & party doing thereon what to Justice appertaines according to ye Lawes of the Kingdom of England and this our Colony & Dominion of Virginia with power likewise to you & every of you to take deposisions and examinacons upon Oath for ye better manifestation of ye truth in all such matters & causes cominge before you and to keep or cause to be kept all orders of Court, Orders of Councill & Proclamacons directed to you or comeinge to your hands from us or from our Governr: & Comandr: in Cheife for ye time being & our Councell of State and to punish ye offenders according to ye Lawes of our Kingdom of England & of this our Colony & Dominion of Virga: And further to keep or cause ye Clerk of your Court to keep Records of all Judgments, Rules, Orders decided and agreed upon by you or any four or more of you whereof ye JNO: CATLETT, WM. MOSELEY, THOMAS EDMONDSON, EDWARD THOMAS, FRANCIS TALIAFERRO & BERNARD GAINES shall be one And further we comand you and every one of you that you diligently intend ye keeping of ye Peace, Statutes of our Kingdom of England and ye Lawes of this Colony & Dominion & all & singular other ye premisses; We do also by vertue of these pr:sents comand ye Sheriff of ye sd County of Essex that at those certain days wch: the Law doth appoint that he cause to come before you or any four or more of you JNO: CATLETT, WM. MOSELEY, THOMAS EDMONDSON, EDWARD THOMAS, FRANCIS TALIAFERRO & BERNARD GAINES shall be one such & so many good & lawfull men of this Bayliwick whom ye hath in ye matters may be ye better known & enquired of. Witness in Justice well beloved FRANCIS NICHOLSON Esqr. our Lt. Govr., Genl., of this our Colony & Dominion of Virga: at JAMES TOWN under ye Seale of our Colony ye 8th day of June in ye Eleventh year of our Reign Ano Dom 1699

A Comission of ye Peace for this County FR: NICHOLSON

E. JENNINGS, Dept. Secry.

Truly recorded Test FRANCIS MERIWETHER, Cl Cur

pp. 1-2 William the Third by the grace of God of England, Scotland, France & Ireland do &c. to JNO: CATLETT, WM. MOSELEY, THO: EDMONDSON, EDWARD THOMAS, FRANCIS TALIAFERRO, BERNARD GAINES, ROBERT BROOKE, JNO. BATTAILE, JNO. TALIAFERRO, JAMES BOUGHAN, FRANCIS GOULDMAN, RICHD. COVINGTON, DANL. DOBYNS & ROBERT PAYNE Gentlemen Greeting. Know yee that whereas we have constituted & appointed you Justices of the Peace for Essex County we do therefore authorize & appoint that you JNO: CATLETT, WM. MOSELEY, THO: EDMONDSON, EDWARD THOMAS, FRANCIS TALIAFERRO & BERNARD GAINES haveing first taken ye Oathes appointed by Act of Parliamt. to be tken in place of the Oathes of Allegience & Supremacy ye Test together with Oath of duely executinge of Justices of ye Peace menconed in an Act of Parliamt: entituled an Act for ye better security of his Mats. Royall person & (a copy of wch: you herewith receive) which ye sd ROBT. BROOKE & JNO. BATTAILE or any two Commissioners abovenamed are hereby required & impowered to give & administer you unto ye abovesd. Justices every of them in ye Commission abovenamed Oathes appointed by Act of Parliamt. to be taken instead of the Oathes of Allegiance & Supremacy together with Oathes of duely executing ye Office of a Justice of ye Peace & of ye p:formance of wch: you are to make due return to our Secrs. Office at JAMES CITY on ye Sixth day of ye next Genll. Court Witness our trusty & well beloved FRANCIS NICHOLSON Esqr. our Lt. & Govr. Genl. of our Colony & Dominion of Virginia at JAMES TOWN and ye Seale of our Colony ye Eighth day of June in ye Eleventh yeare of our Reign Ano Dom 1699

A Dedimus for Administring ye Oaths & Test &c. FR: NICHOLSON
to ye Justices of ye Peace for Essex County
E. JENINGS Dept. Secry:
Truely recorded Test FRANCIS MERIWETHER, Cl Cur

p. 2 Att a Councill helde at JAMES CITY June ye 21. 1699
Present
His Excellency in Councill

Ordered that ye Comrs. of every County within this Dominion do as soon as possible returne to ye Councill Office at JAMES CITY a exact acct. of what Publick or Private meetings of any other RELIGIONS then ye Church of England as by Law established are in their respective Countyes where they are kept, how longe they have beenkept, how lycensed, how many & what persons report thereto, what particular Religion they are of, how their Preachers are quallified & whether any wandering Strangers come into their Counties as Preachers or upon any other pretence of Religion whatsoever

B. HARRISON
Truely recorded Test FRANCIS MERIWETHER, Cl Cur

p. 2 Att a Councill held at JAMES CITY June y 21st 1699
Present
His Excellency in Councill

Whereas his Majty: by his Royall Instructions to his Excellency hath directed that no SCHOOL MASTER be henceforth permitted to come from England to keep SCHOOL wthin: this Colony of Virga: without ye Lycense of ye Lord Bishop of LONDON and that no other person now in this Colony or that shall come hither from other parts be admitted to keep SCHOOL without his Excellencys Lycense first had, therefore ordered that ye severall County Courts within this Dominion do as soon as conveniently may return to ye Councills Office a p:ticular Acct. what SCHOOLS are in their respective Counties & whether ye Masters thereof are Lycensed according to ye sd Instructions & to recommend such as are fit and capable for that Imploymt. tht they may be lycensed accor-

dingly, wch: Lycense are to be granted them without any fee or any other Charge
B. HARRISON
Truely recorded Test FRANCIS MERIWETHER, Cl Cur

p. 2 Att a Councill held at JAMES CITY June ye 7th 1699
Present
His Excellency in Councill
Ordered that all Commissioned & non Commissioned Officers of ye Militia, Excheatrs: Coroners, Commissors: & other Officers in this Dominion at their Admissin into their severall Offices respectively do take ye Oaths appointed by Act of Parliamt. to be taken instead of ye Oaths of Supremacy & Allegiance & Subscribe ye Test & Associacon appointed by Act of Parliamt., therefore ordered that Mr. Attorney Genll. do prepare a Commicon for the purpose impoweringe such persons as his Excellency shall think fit to appoint to administer ye sd Oathes, Test & Associacon as aforesd.
B. HARRISON
Truely recorded Test FRANCIS MERIWETHER, Cl Cur

p. 3 Att A Councill helde at JAMES CITY June ye 22d 1699
Present
His Excellency in Councill
Mr. Attorney Genll. according to order reported his Opinion conerning Probates and Admrcons. & Lycences for Marriages in these words following:
May it please yor: Excellency:
I am humbly of opinion that Probates of Wills, Letters of Admistrcons ought to be signed by yor: Excellency & by no other, it being a Judiciall Act in wch: no Deputy can be appointed but as to Lycenses for Marriages I am of opinion yor: Excellency may depute such persons you shall think fit to grant ye same being thereto authorised by ye Lawes of his Majts. Colony & Dominion of Virga; Whereupon its ordered that for ye future, Probates of Wills & Letters of Administrcons. be prepared by ye Clerks of ye severall County Courts where ye same shall be granted respectively transmitted to JAMES CITY to be signed by his Excellency according to ye ancient Lawes & practice of this his Majts. Colony & Dominion & that no other person do pr:sume hereafter to signe any Probate or Commission of Admr. as of late hath been acted
B. HARRISON
Truely recorded Test FRANCIS MERIWETHER, Cl Cur

p. 3 Att a Councill helde at JAMES CITY June ye 22d 1699
Present
His Excellency in Councill
Mr. Attorney Genll. according to Order haveing reported his opinion as ye method of proceeding in relacon to Escheate Landes in these words following;
May it please your Excellency:
I have considered ye Lawes & Statutes of England relateing to Escheats offered therein severall rules established:
1. That a return of all Enquests of Escheat ought to be made by ye Escheatr: within one month after ye Office found
2. That all Enquests ought to be taken in Towns & open places & by good & Substantial men & openly by Indenture between ye Escheatr: & Jury
3. That no grant be made of any land seized into ye Kings Hdns. unto Office found & that all grants before Office found should be void

4. That a moneths time after ye return of ye Enquest ought to be allowed for that thos that have right to traverse ye sd Escheat before any Grant be made thereof. I also find that his late Majty. King Charles ye Second by his Charter granted to this Colony & Dominion of Virga: dated ye 10th day of October in ye 28th yeare of his Reign did himselfe confirm that all lands possest by any Subject inhabiting in Virginia which die or should escheat should or might be enjoyed by such Inhabitant or Possessor his heirs & assignes for ever paying Two pounds of Tobacco composition for every (acre) of land so escheated; So that upon ye whole matter with Submission to yor: Excellency & Honble. Board, I humbly propose ye following method of Escheats as ye most agreeable to ye Lawes of England his late Maj. Royall Charter & most suitable to ye Circumstances of his Majts. Colony & Dominion

1. That upon reasonble suggestion or upon ye knowledge of ye Escheatr: himselfe any land Escheates to his Majty. a Writt do issue in ye nature of a Mandamus or directed to ye Escheatr: comanding him to find ye Office by ye Enquest by twelve men as ye Statutes of England direct

2. That no enquest be taken but in Publick & open places and that notice be given by ye Escheatr: by note under his hand set up at ye Court House of ye County where ye land doth lye upon Court day of ye time & place of takeing ye Enquest before any Enquest shall be made

3. That a return of ye Enquest into ye Secretaries Office shall be made within one moneth at farthest after ye Enquest taken

4. That no grant be made of any lands Escheated to his Majty. untill Office found

5. That a convenient time be allowed after Office found to increase ye Escheat of any lands of a grant be made thereof

6. That no Possessr: in his own right should have ye precedence of all Claims provided he make his ( ) known by Petr: to yor: Excellency within such time after Office found as shall be thought convenient

7. That ye Grantee may pay so much p Ct. for composition for ye same to his Majtyes as that he thought reasonable thereupon ordered that in all time (torn) at ( ) of ye several Counties of this his Majties. Colony & Dominion in (torn)

p. 3 William ye Third by ye grace of God, King of England, Scotland, France & Ireland Defender of ye faith &c., to JNO: CATLETT, WM. MOSELEY, THO: EDMONDSON, FRA: TALIAFERRO, BER: GAINES, ROBT. BROOKE, JNO. BATTAILE, JNO. TALIAFERRO, JAMES BOUGHAN, FRA: GOULDMAN, RICHD. COVINGTON, DANL. DOBYNS & ROBT. PAYNE Gent., greeting We Com and require you & any four of you to be one to be summoned all ye Malitia Officers in ye County of Essex to next Court helde for ye sd County or to any suceeding Court then & there to Administer to ye sd Malitia Officers & every of them & others appointed by Act of Parliamt. to be instead of ye Oathes of Allegiance & Supremacy ye Test & ye Associacion menconed in an Act of Parliamt. of ye 7th & 8th years of our Reign entituled an Act for ye better security of his Majties. Royall person & Governmt. of ye p:formance of which ye are to make due return under your hands & seales to our Secrys. Office at JAMES CITTY on ye Sixth day of ye next Genll. Court Witness our trusty & well beloved FRANCIS NICHOLSON Esqr. our Lt. & Govr: Genll. of our Colony & Dominion of Virga: at JAMES TOWN under ye Seale of our Colony this 22d day of June 1699 in ye Eleventh year of our Reign

Commission to swear ye Malitia Officers in FR: NICHOLSON
Essex County C. C. THACKER
Truly recorded FRANCIS MERIWETHER Cl Cur

p. William the third by ye grace of God of England, Scotland, France & Ireland,
3 Defendr. of ye faith &c. to JNO. CATLETT, WM. MOSELEY, THO: EDMONDSON, FRA. TALIAFERRO, BER: GAINES, ROBT: BROOKE, JNO. BATTAILE, JNO. TALIAFERRO, JAMES BAUGHAN, FRA: GOULDMAN, RICH: COVINGTON, DANL. DOBYNS & ROBT. PAYNE Gent. greeting. We do authorize & appoint you or any four or more of you whereof any of you to be one at ye next Court to held for the County of Essex or at any succeeding Court to administer ye Oathes appointed by Act of Parliamt. to be taken instead of ye Oathes of Allegiance & Supremacy Test & ye Associacon menconed in an Act of Parliamt. made in ye 7th & 8th years of our Reign entituled An Act for ye Better Security of his Mats: Royall Person & Governmt., & ye Oathes for ye due execution of ye severall offices of ye Sheriff, Under Sheriff & Bayliffs of ye sd County, to ye several Constables & Head Borroughs in ye sd County, to ye Clerke of ye sd County Court & his Deputy, to ye several Coroners, Escheaters, Surveyors their Deputies in ye sd County, ye INDIAN INTERPRETER, if there be any of ye p:son in such of wch: you are to make return under your hands & seales to our Secrys. Office at JAMES CITY Witness our trusty & well beloved FRA: NICHOLSON Esqr. our Lt. & Govr. Genll. of our Colony & Dominion in Virga: at JAMES TOWN undr: ye Seale of our Colony this 22d day of June 1699 in ye eleventh year of our Reign

A Dedimus for Admstring. ye Oathes Test & Associacon of ye Civil Officers in Essex County FRA: NICHOLSON

C: C: THACKER

Truely recorded Test FRANCIS MERIWETHER, Cl Cur

p. KNOW ALL MEN by these pr:sents that I TIMOTHY WYBERG of WHITEHAVEN have
3 named Mr. ROBT. MOSELEY of Rappa: my true & lawfull Attorney for me & in my name to receive debts as (p contra) to me due & by sd persons giveing & hereby granting unto my said Attorney my full power to execute all things in ye Law as shall be necessary for recovering ye debts and acquittances & other discharges in my name to do in ye premisses as I myselfe might or could do being present confirming all whatsoever my sd Attorney shall lawfully do In Witness whereof I have hereunto set my hand & seale ye 17th day of June 1699

Signed sealed & delivered in ye p:sence of

JERE: LOWES TIMOTHY WYBERGH

HAMLETT ROBINSON

Proved in Essex County Court ye 10th day of Augt. 1699 by Oath of JERE: LOWES

Truely recorded Test FRANCIS MERIWETHER, Cl Cur

p. KNOW ALL MEN by these pr:sents that I JOHN WILLIS & MARY WILLIS my Wife of
3 ye Parish of (torn) in ye County of Essex for ye sum of Four thousand pounds of lawfull tobacco in hand delivering by THOMAS RAMSEY of ye same Parish & County we ye sd JOHN WILLIS & MARY WILLIS do hereby sell unto said THO: RAMSEY his heirs assignes forever Two hundred eighty nine acres & fifty perches of land being in ye Parish of Sittingburn & County of Essex and on ye branches of OCCUPATION CREEK, it being part & parcell of a tract of land granted to JAMES COGHILL deced by Patent bearing date in Aprill ye 19th in year of our Lord 1667 and left to MARY COGHILL, his Daughter, & now ye Wife of ye sd JOHN WILLIS To have and to hold ye sd Two hundred eighty nine acres & fifty perches of land begining at a marked red Oake standing on ye Eastward side of ye head of a Valley buting on ye line of DANLL. NOELL by a PATH that goeth to his house & runeth thence South to a marked white Oake standing in Mr. SAML. BLUMFEILDs line & thence along ye land of BLUMFEILDs line West to a marked red Oak &

thence along the sd BLUMFEILDs line South to a Stake standing as a Corner tree in ye sd BLUMFEILDs line & corner to a line devideth between ye other moyety of the sd land by Patent granted as aforesd. & thence runeth West to ye head line of ye whole Devident & thence North East to a marked red Oak standing in Mr. PAGEs line, & thence along ye sd PAGEs line to ye first menconed Station to him ye sd THO: RAMSEY ye sd land with all its rights belonging against ye sd JNO: WILLIS & MARY WILLIS our selves our heirs & will warrant at all times forever hereafter lawfully & quietly hve ye sd land from denial or disturbance of ye sd JNO: WILLIS & MARY WILLIS their heirs or assignes In Witness we ye sd JNO: WILLIS & MARY WILLIS do hereunto put our hands & seales this 10th day of December Ano Dom 1698

Signed sealed & delivered in ye pr:sence of us

CORNELIUS NOELL — JOHN I WILLIS
JEREM: PARKER — MARY M WILLIS

Acknowledged in Essex County Court ye 10th day of Augt: 1699 & truely recorded

pp. KNOW ALL MEN by these presents that I JOHN WILLIS of ye County of Essex do
3- bind make over & confirm unto THO: RAMSEY of ye County aforesd. his heirs &
4 assignes every part & parcell of my land lying & being in ye County of RICH-
MOND on ye side of Rappa: River that doth any waie belong or appeare to belong to me & for true p:formance I do bind my selfe my heirs by these pr:sents Witness my hand & seale this tenth of December 1699

The Condicon of this present obligacon is such that if ye above bounden JNO. WILLIS his heirs do at all times forever well & truely observe all ye Agreemts. made in one Deed of Bargaine & Sale bearing equal date with these pr:sents betweene above bounden JNO: WILLIS & MARY his Wife & ye above named THO: RAMSEY & in the behalfe of ye sd JNO: WILLIS & MARY his Wife ought to be p:formed without any fraud that then this present obligacon shall be void else to remaine in full force

Signed sealed & delivered in ye pr:sence of us

BARTHO: VAWTER, — JOHN I WILLIS
RICHARD R JACKSON

Acknowledged in Essex County Court ye 10th day of Aug: 1699 & truely recorded
Test FRANCIS MERIWETHER, Cl Cur

pp. HENRY ARKWELL. Dr. 1698. Contra: By ye sd ARKWELLs Estate 5115
3- To 5 pair of mens shoes at 70 p; to 2 pair of Lads ditto; to 2 pair of mens ditto;
4 to a quart of Brandy, to ye mending one pair of shoes, to arrears due in 1697, to
tobacco paid ye Widow DUCKSBURY & him WM. JONES for cleaning ye beding; to my trouble of looking after ye Stock, to my trouble of burying of him, To JNO. RENNALLS Bill, to an order past to BER: GAINES; to 2 years rent paid Capt. BROOKES; to JOSHUA DAVIS by order of Court, to EDWD. SKRIMSHER by Order of Court 4559
To Clerks fees Errors Excepted p THOMAS TINSLEY
Delivd. in Essex County Court ye 10th day of Augt. 1699 & truely recorded according to Order of Court Test FRANCIS MERIWETHER, Cl Cur

p. IN YE NAME OF GOD Amen ye Eighth day of October in ye yeare of our Lord God
4 1698 I JONATHAN GRILLS in ye County of Essex in ye County of Virga: being
very sick weak of body but of perfect mind & memory thanks be given unto God, I do make & ordaine this my last Will & Testamt. in manner & forme following, That is to say, first & cheifly I give my Soul into the hands of Almighty God who gave it me and my body I comend to ye Earth to be decently buryed in Christian buryal at ye discretion

of my Ex:Ex: nothing doubting but that at ye generall resurrection I shall receive ye same againe by ye mighty power of God, as touching my worldly Estate wherewith it hath pleased God to bless me I give & devise & bequeath ye same in manner & form following that is to say; I give unto my Loveing Daughter, ANN GRILLS, one tract of land containing One hundred & twenty acres lying in ye FOREST in ye County of Essex aforesd., one Mare of three years old, a good young Cow & calfe, a sowe Pigg, a flock bed & blankets & rugg & bolster, three pewter dishes, a pott & pott hooks, six spoons, a payle, a frying pann, two plates & a Porringer, a sifter & two chairs ye sd things to be truely paid out of my Estate unto my said Daughter, ANN, at ye age of Sixteen years or day of Marriage, but in case she dyes before my Wife, then what I have in land or goods I leave unto my Wife, ANN GRILLS, & her heirs but in case my Wife dyes and she leaves my Daughter & her two Sons, FRANCIS & WM. PEIRCY, then all my land lying on PISSCUTTAWAYA CREEKE & goods to be equally divided betwixt them & their heirs lawfully begotten of their own bodyes & in case either of them dyes without issue then it is my true intent & meaning that ye longest liver of them shall have is remaininge of my Estate reall or personall to them or him or their heires forever

Item. It is my will that my said Wife, ANN GRILLES, after my decease shall have ye liberty to remaine on ye sd Plantacon of PISCATAWAY CREEK as long as she lives & to have use of ye sd household goods Stock provided that she payes my said Daughter the sd Legacies that are above menconed And of this my last Will & Testamt. I make my beloved Wife my full & sole Exex. & I do hereby revoke & annull all & every other former Wills legacies bequests & Exers. by me otherwise beforenamed, willed & bequeathed ratifying & confirming this & none other to be my last Will & Testamt. In Witness whereof I have hereto set my hand & seale ye day & year above written

Signed sealed & delivered published & declared
by ye sd JONA: GRILLS as his Last Will & Testamt. in ye p:sence of — JONATHAN GRILLES
ST. JOHN SHROPSHIRE
ELIZ: SHROPSHIRE, WILLIAM MARCHANT

Prov'd in Essex County Court by ye Oath of ST. JOHN SHROPSHIRE & WM. MARCHANT ye 10th day of Augt. 1699 FRANCIS MERIWETHER, Cl Cur

p. 4 KNOW ALL MEN by these pr:sents that I JOHN BRAISIER & KATHERINE his Wife, JONATHAN FISHER & HENRY GOARE are helde & firmly bound unto his Majts: Justices of ye Peace for ye County of Essex in the sum of Twenty thousand pounds of tobo: & caske for ye true payment we bind our selves Witness our hands & seales this 10th day of Augt. Ano: Dom: 1699

The Condicon of this obligacon is that if ye above bound JNO: BRAISIER & ANN his Wife who at a Court held for this County this day obtained a Probate of ye last Will & Testament of JONATHAN GRILLS deced shall & do from time to time & at all times hereafter to all intents & purposes p:form & fullfil ye sd Will fully pay & satisfie all such Legatees as therein are expressed & doe perform all & whatsoever ye Law enjoynes in such cases, that then ye above obligacon to be void otherwise to stand & remaine of full force

Signed Sealed & dd. in pr:sence of us
FRANCIS MERIWETHER,
WILL: YOUNG

JOHN I BRAISIER
JONATHAN FISHER
HEN: GOARE
ANN C BRAISIER

Truely recorded Test
FRANCIS MERIWETHTER, Cl Cur

pp. 4-5 THIS INDENTURE made ye fifth day of August in ye year One thousand Six hundred Ninety & nine between WM: HARPER of ye Parish of Cittenborne in ye County of Essex within ye Colony of Virga:, Planter, (Son & heir of WM. HARPER late of ye same Parish & County, Planter, deced) of ye one part & THOS: GREGSON of ye Parish & County aforesd. Gent., of ye other part. Witnesseth that for ye sum of fifty pds. of lawfull money of England unto ye sd WM. HARPER in hand well & truely paid by ye sd THO: GREGSON he ye sd WM. HARPER (party to these pr:sents) hath sold unto ye sd THO: GREGSON his heirs & assignes One hundred & fifty acres of land being in ye Parish of Sittenbourne & County of Essex aforesd. formerly called RAPPAHANNOCK County bounded as followeth, beginning at a red Oake upon a point by a little Creek proceeding out of OCCUPATION CREEKE buting upon ye land formerly surveyed for RICHD. COLEMAN to ye outside line of land of WM. HALL paralleli to wch: it runeth South East to a red Oake being a Corner tree of ye sd HALLs land by ye aforesd. Creekes side from which to ye first menconed red Oake, South West by West in which ye sd bounds is included the said land being formerly granted unto ye sd WM. HARPER deced by Patent dated ye twentieth day of Febry: 1662 & by him deserted and granted unto Major JNO. WEIR by Order of ye Court & by Patent bearing date ye second day of October 1667 and by ye sd Majr. JOHN WEIRE assigned unto ye sd WM. HARPER deced by an Endorsemt. of ye sd Patent bearing date ye fifth day of December 1667 & now doth of right belong unto ye sd WM. HARPER (party to these pr:sents) as Son & heir of ye sd WM. HARPER deced as aforesaid, with all houses buildings stables tobacco houses orchards profits & appurtenances to ye sd tract of land belonging, To have & to hold ye sd land and all ye premisses unto ye sd THO: GREGSON his heirs & assignes forever And that he ye sd THO: GREGSON his heirs & assignes may at all time forever hereafter peaceably & quietly possess all ye before granted p:misses without denial of ye sd WM. HARPER (party to these pr:sents) his heirs or any other persons aforesaid. In Witness whereof ye parties first above named their hands & seales have sett

Signed sealed & delivered in ye presence of

RO: BROOKE, JOHN PEATLE, WM. HARPER

SAML. THACKER, THO: WINSLOW

Acknowledged in Essex County Court ye 10th day of Augt: 1699

Memorand: That full & peaceable possession was given & delivered by WM. HARPER unto THO: GREGSON to hold to him forever accordinge to ye intent of ye Indenture within written, ye fifth day of Augt: 1699

In presence of RO: BROOKE, JOHN PEATLE

SAML. THACKER, THO: WINSLOW

Acknowledged by ye sd W. HARPER in Essex County Court ye 10th day of Augt. 1699 & recorded FRANCIS MERIWETHER, Cl Cur

KNOW ALL MEN by these pr:sents that I WM. HARPER of ye Parish of Sittenburne in County of Essex within ye Colony of Virga:, Planter, (Son & heir of WM. HARPER of ye same Parish & County, Planter, deced) am firmly bound unto THO: GREGSON of ye same Parish & County in ye sum of One hundred pounds of good & lawfull money of England to be paid I bind myselfe dated ye fifth day of Augt. in ye year of our Lord God One thousand six hundred ninety nine

The Condicon of this obligacon is that if the above bounden WM. HARPER well & truely keep all condicons on ye behalfe of ye sd WM. HARPER in one pair of Indentures bearing date with these pr:sents made between ye sd WM. HARPER of ye one part and THO: GREGSON of ye other part, Then this obligacon to be void or else to remaine in full force Sealed & delivered in ye pr:sence of

RO: BROOKE, JOHN PEATLE, WM: HARPER

SAML. THACKER, THO: WINSLOW

Acknowledged in Essex County Court ye 10th day of Augt: 1699 & recorded

p. 5 Ess: ss MARY JEWEL aged fifty eight years or thereabouts being examined & sworne deposeth that Ms. HANAH TOMLIN, Daughter of Mr. ROBT. TOMLIN late of this County deced borne ye 21st day of December in ye year 1674 and that she died in Aprill in ye year 1698 & further saith not

MARY M JEWEL

Sworne to in Essex County Court ye 10th day of Augt: 1699 Test FRANCIS MERIWETHER, Cl Cur

p. 5 Essex ss. ELIZABETH PLEY aged fifty six years or thereabouts being examined & sworne deposeth that Ms. HANNAH TOMLIN late of this County deced, (Daughter to Mr. ROBT. TOMLIN late of Essex County deced) was borne either ye 21st or 22d day of December in ye year 1674 and that she died in Aprill in ye year 1698 & further saith not

ELIZABETH PLEY

Sworne to in Essex County Court ye 10th day of Augt: 1699 Test FRANCIS MERIWETHER, Cl Cur

p. 5 Wee the Subsbribers do praise the Estate of JOHN EYLES as followeth: Old & new pewter, one feather bed & rugg & coverlid, parsell of table linnen, razor, one hone, two knives, parcell of Carpenters tooles, earthen ware, one hand saw, one yearling Colt, a sadle & forme, four thousand nailes, 2 ladles, one smoothing iron, parcell of old lumber, two chests, pott rack, spining wheel & one hatt, bed stead & a pair of stilliards, two feather pillows, three wedges, a hand saw, a hammer, a kettle, a butter pott, a old flock bed, bolster pillow, five cowes, two heifers, three yearlings Sum: totall: 31...11...00

HENRY h WOODNETT THOMAS GREENE
ANDREW A DUDIN WILLIAM HARDING

Presented by JAMES OSMAN Exer. of JNO: ILES deced upon Oath at a Court held for Essex County ye 10th day of Augt. 1699 & recorded FRANCIS MERIWETHER, Cl Cur

p. 6 By one Mare, two cowes & calves, one feather bed, a flock bed & furniture, to a small chest, a parcell of trayes & a sifter, two towells & pillow beer; a parcell of pewter, one rasor, fraying pain, smothing iron, one pott & hooks, a pair of deer skins, one old Gunn, one old saddle & parcell of lumber.

July ye 25th 1699 Then in obedience to an order of Court bearing date ye 10th day of Janry: 1699 we ye Subscribers being first sworne before Mr. THO: EDMONDSON have accordingly inventoryed & appraised ye Estate of JNO: CLARKE

Presented by MICHAEL RICE & (?LUEN) his Wife (Admrs. of JNO. CLARKE deced) upon Oath at a Court held for Essex County ye 10th day of Augt. 1699 & truely recorded

THOM: T WOOD
JOHN FARGESON
FRANCIS BROWNE
JA: FULLERTON

P. 6 At a Court held for Essex County June y 19th 1699 an Order being past for ye Inventorying and Appraisinge the Estate of WARWICK GRAY deced, We ye Subscribers in obedience to that Order have to the best of our Judgmt. appraised & inventoryed ye same in manner following:

Two cows & one horse, one yearling Cow calfe, one horse, one cart & wheels & harness, one Boat, one Cattaile bed & pair of sheets, one blanket & bolster, one gunn, parsell of old cloathes, iron pott, parsell of old pewter, old iron, parsell of Lumber, one Couch, halfe bushell of Salt, caske & one grind stone, one chair, one Bible. TOTAL 5114

WM. GANNOCKE THO: T THORPE
CHARLES BROWNE THO: ꝏ TINSLEY

SAML. JOHNSON dd. to ye Estate of WARWICK GREY; WM. PRICE delivered to ye Estate of WARWICK GREY. Presented by JOSIAH SHIPP (Exer. of WARWICK GREY deced) upon Oath at a Court held for Essex County ye 10th day of Augutst 1699 & truely recorded

Sworne by me BER: GAINES

p. 6 The Deposicon of HENRY WAINWRIGHT aged 26 years or thereabouts sworne saith that yor: Depont. did hear JNO. CARRELL say that he had sold a FLATT to Mr. ROBT. COLEMAN and that my Master, Capt. THO: LETTENBEY should deliver ye sd FLATT to ye sd COLEMAN when ye sd LETTENBEY had done wth: her wch: he did & further saith not.

HENRY WAINWRIGHT

Sworne to in Essex County Court ye 10th day of Augt. 1699 & truely recorded

pp. 6-7 THIS INDENTURE made ye 10th day of Augt. in ye year of our Lord God One thousand six hundred ninety nine Between THO: MEADOWS of ye County of Essex (together with SUSANNA my Wife) within ye Colony of Virga:, Planter, Son & heir of JOHN MEADOWS, late of ye same County, Planter, deced of the one part and GEO: LOYD of ye Parish of Cittenburne in ye County aforesd., Planter, of ye other part Witnesseth that for ye sum of Seven thousand & five hundred pounds of good sound merchantable tobacco unto ye sd THO: MEADOWS in hand well & truly paid the sd THO: MEADOWS hath granted unto ye sd GEO: LOYD his heirs & assignes forever all that devident of land containing Five hundred & fifty acres being in the Parish of St. Maries & County of Essex aforesd., formerly called RAPPAHANNOCK County, bounded as followeth, begining at an Oake Corner tree in THOMAS GRIFFING (upon ye branches of PEWMANSEND and on ye South side of ye Maine River & on ye East side of a forke of the said River) thence up ye Maine Run to a marked Beech corner tree that ye division line begineth at that pasteth WM. GANNOCK & THO: MEADOWS, thence South West to a marked white Oake standing in ye devision line, thence North West to a marked white Oake, thence East to a marked Hickory standing in ye sd Division Line, thence East to a marked Hickory standing in CHRISTOPHER MANs line & along ye sd MANs line West to a marked Dogwood; thence South West to a sweet Gum corner to sd THO: GRIFFING & thence along sd GRIFFINGs North to ye first menconed Station, the said land being part of a Patent bearing date ye 17th day of April 1664 and now doth of right belong unto ye sd THO: MEADOWS as Son & heir of ye sd JNO: MEADOWS deced as aforesd., wth: all houses buildings fences barns woods swamps & appurtenances whatsoever belonging (Now Know yee that Fifty acres of this land hereby granted is that which is excepted in ye Deed of Gift as I ye sd MEADOWS gave to WM. GANNOCK as by Record may appear) To have & to hold unto ye sd GEO: LOYD his heirs & assignes forever and the said THO: MEADOWS & SUSANNA his Wife will warrant & forever defend And also that GEO: LOYD his heirs & assignes shall possess the said land without any trouble of ye sd THO: MEADOWS & SUSANNA his Wife their heirs or any other persons wt:soever

Sealed & delivered in ye presence of

ROBT. COLEMAN, THOMAS T MEADOWS
JOHN PEATLE, PHIL: PARR SUSANNAH X MEADOWS

Acknowledged & right of Dower relinquished in Essex County ye 11th day of Augt. 1699 & truely recorded Test FRANCIS MERIWETHER, Cl Cur

KNOW ALL MEN that I THO: MEADOWS of ye County of Essex, Son & heir of JNO. MEADOWS late of ye same County, Planter, am firmly bound unto GEO: LOYD of ye Parish of Cittenburne in sd County in ye sum of Fifteen thousand pounds of good sound merchantable tobo: dated ye 10th day of Augt. 1699

The Condicon of this obligacon is if THO: MEADOWS his heirs truely observe all articles contained in Indenture made to abovenamed GEO: LOYD in all things then this obligacon to be void or else to remain in full power

Sealed & delivered in pr:sence of

ROBT. COLEMAN, THOMAS T MEADOWS

JOHN PEATLE, PHIL: PARR

Acknowledged in Essex County Court ye 11th day of Augt. 1699

p. 7 KNOW ALL MEN by these presents that we THO: BARNET & JANE his Wife, SAML. PERRY & JEFFRY DYER of ye County of Essex are firmly bound unto his Majties. Justices of ye Peace in ye sum of Twenty thousand pounds of tobo: & caske this 11th day of Augt: 1699

The Condicon of ye above obligacon is that if the above bound THO: BARNET & JANE his Wife, Admrs. of JNO: POWELL deced, do make a perfect inventory of all ye goods chattels rights & credits of ye sd deced wch: shall come to ye hands & do exhibit to ye next Court & make oath thereto & pay such persons respectively at ye Court p:suant to Law shall appoint, then ye above obligacon to be void otherwise to remain in force

Signed sealed & delivered in ye presence of us

FRANCIS MERIWETHER, THOMAS B BURNET

ROBT. MOSELEY SAMLL. PARRY

JEFFRY I DYER

JANE I BARNET

Truely recorded FRANCIS MERIWETHER, Cl Cur

p. 7 In Obedience to an Order of Essex County Court we ye Subscribers being sworne by RICHD. COVINGTON have appraised such of ye Estate of RICHD. LAKELAND deced as was pr:sented to us by Mr. WM. YOUNG, Admr., as followeth, Tobo:

To 1 Camlet Coat & vest & kersey Coat; two old shirts, 4 old wastecoates & a neckcloth; 2 old Coates, 1 old hatt, 1 pr. of old leather breeches, 2 pr. of old stockins, 2 pr. of linen breeches, small chest, 3 old books & some old tobo: reced from ye Parish, HEN. GOSSELLs Bill due, due from Mr. ROBT. COLEMAN Total 1440

Sworne to before me this second day of Augt. 1699 HENRY WOODNUT

RICHD: COVINGTON ANDREW DUDING

Febry. 3d. 1699 p WILL: YOUNG deced by WM. YOUNG upon Oath at a Court held for Essex County ye 11th day of Augt. 1699 truely recorded

p. 8 Essex County July ye 12th 1699

In Obedience to an Order of ye sd County Court ye 10th of June 1699, We ye Subscribers being sumoned & first sworne before Mr. RICHD. COVINGTON have met at ye House of ye deced & have Inventoryed & appraised such part of ye deceds Estate as was produced before us in money as followeth (vizt.)

4 Cows & calves, 1 steer six years old, 1 steer five years old, 5 barren Cows, 5 yearlings, 2 heifers 2 years old, 1 steer 2 years old, 2 bulls, 2 horses, 1 old feather bed blankets & rugg, 1 old bed tick & 1 old rugg, 2 old flock ditto; 1 broad cloth Coat & breeches, 1 kersey Coat, 1 pr. of linen draws & 1 felt hatt old, 2 old coates & 1 old wastcoat, 3 sheets, a parcell of old table linen, 2 dressed deer skins, 2 old chests, 2 looking glasses, 1 hone & 2 razors,

parcell of old Carpendrs: & Coopers tooles, a parcell of old pewter, iron potts & hooks, 2 old saddles & a pad & a bridle, 2 old gunns, To 1500 lbs. mix Nailes, 1 baile paile

By JNO. WATERS Debt in money 15/6. By a bed stead, by Debts due in tobacco; WM YOUNG dect, JNO. WEBSTER debt, HEN: GOSLIN debt; ELIZA: GRIGORY Christian Negro (170) Total 1960 tobacco

p us THOMAS GREENE HENRY WOODNUT
ANDREW /D DUDING WILLIAM HARDING

Sworne before me this 12th day of July 1699 RICH: COVINGTON

Presented by WM. DURHAM & SARAH, his Wife, Exex. of JNO: MITCHELL, Exr. of JNO. CLARKE deced upon Oath at a Court held for Essex County ye 10th day of Augt. 1699 truely recorded

p. 8 KNOW ALL MEN by these pr:sents that I JOHN PICKET of ye County of Essex am firmly bound unto his Maties: Justices of ye Peace for ye County aforesd. in ye full sum of Two thousand pounds of tobo: & caske for ye wch: payment I bind myselfe witness my hand this 11th day of Augt. 1699

The Condicon of ye above obligacon is that whereas ye above bounded JNO. PICKET hath a Servant man named JNO; DOPSON who hath abused MARY BOUGHAN, Widow, Now if ye sd JNO. DOPSON do from time to time & dureing ye time of ye sd JNO: DOPSONs service behave himselfe & keep his Majties. Peace in all things as an honest man should or ought to do towards ye sd MARY BOUGHAN, then this obligacon to be void or else to remain in full force

JNO: PICKET
HENRY H PICKET

Acknowledged by JNO: PICKET & HEN: PICKET in Essex County Court ye 11th day of Augt. 1699 & truely recorded Test FRANCIS MERIWETHER, Cl Cur

p. 8 ROBT. COLEMAN. This is to request you to appear for me & in my behalfe to answer Mr. CHARLES TALIAFERRO in an accon now depending between ye sd TALIAFERRO & me ye Subscriber & what my said Attorney shall act & do in ye sd case I do ratifie & allow to be as valid in ye Law as if I myselfe were there present. Witness my hand this 10th day of Augt. 1699

SAMLL. SALLIS

Truely recorded Test FRANCIS MERIWETHER, Cl Cur

p. 8 KNOW ALL MEN by these presents that we JNO: PARKER, MARTHA PARKER, THO: GREGSON & ELIZA: PLEY of ye County of Essex are firmly bound unto his Mats: Justices of ye Peace for the County of Essex in ye sum of Twenty thousand pds. of tobo: Witness our hands & seales this 11th day of Augt. 1699

The Condicon of ye above obligacon is that if JNO: PARKER & MARTHA PARKER, Admrs. of SILVANUS TANDY deced do make perfect Inventory of all ye goods chattells & credits of the deced & do make exhibit to ye Court that shall be held for ye sd County of Essex & pay unto such persons as ye Court p:suant to Law shall appoint, then ye above obligacon to be void otherwise to remaine in full force

Signed sealed & delivered in presence of us

FRA: MERIWETHER,
PHIL: PARR

JNO: PARKER
MARTHA M PARKER
THO: GREGSON
ELIZ: PLEY

Truely recorded

p. Upon ye backside of an Attachmt. granted to EDWD. JEFFREYIES agt: ye Estate of
8 ROGER JONES deced made ye following return
Augst. ye 2d. 1699
Executed ye within precept upon ye severall goods & chattells hereof menconed (vizt) a brown two year old heifer, a small starr in her forehead, a black baron cow with a white flanck her ear marked not known & one brown heifer two years old with a starr in her forehead white flanck & tayle on mark, one pair of Smiths Bellows, one small chest & lock, a parcell of old iron, a sledg hammer & small ditto, a small iron pott.

p PHIL: PARR Sub Sher:

Truely recorded Test FRANCIS MERIWETHER, Cl Cur

p. I do hereby authorize & impower Mr. JAMES BOUGHAN of Essex County my true &
8 lawfull Attorney in all such cases as I shall have depending in ye County Court
giveing & granting unto him full power in ye premisses witness my hand this 20th day of Janry: 1698

JAMES BOUGHAN WM. LEIGH
Attorney at Law

Truely recorded Test FRANCIS MERIWETHER, Cl Cur

pp. TO ALL CHRISTIAN PEOPLE to whom these pr:sents shall come I RALPH SPEDE of
8- ye County of RICHMOND send greeting. Knowe yee that I ye sd RALPH SPEDE for
9 divers good causes & especially for Four thousands pds. of tobo: & caske in hand
paid have sold unto PATRICK DORAN of ye abovesd. County One hundred acres of land be more or less being in ye County of Essex & in South Farnham Parish & on ye head of PISCATAWAY CREEK wch: land was bought by me ye sd RALPH SPEED of WM. FREEMAN as may appear by a Deed from under ye FREMANs hand bearing date ye fifth day of Febry: 1693 as followeth: begining at a marked Oake standing by or nigh a branch side arm of ye MIDLE BRANCH called ye BRIGE BRANCH & so runing up ye sd branch to a corner red Oake standing by or nigh ye head of ye sd Branch & thence by a line of marked trees Westerly to a corner red Oake standing by or nigh branch side called CRUMPELL QUARTER BRANCH & thence Southerly by a line of marked trees to a corner red Oake standing by or nigh ye line of JOSEPH GOODRICH, thence Eastwardly along ye abovesd. GOODRICH line to a corner white Oake standing by a branch side and Easterly to a corner white Oake of FRANCIS BROWNEs on a Hill side, so along ye line of ye sd BROWNE to a corner Elme standing by a branch side called ye MIDLE BRANCH & thence down ye sd branch to ye place where it first began. To have & to hold ye said Bargaine of Land & premisses to ye sd PATRICK DORAN & his heires forever wth: all plantacons houseing gardens woods & comodities belonging without molestacon of me ye sd RALPH SPEDE my heirs or assignes, he paying thereof yearly unto our Sovereign Lord ye King usuall due or wch: shall hereafter become due for ye same and ye sd RALPH SPEDE do agree to acknowledge ye sd bargaine of Land at his request as Witness my hand & seale this 9th day of September 1699
Signed sealed & delivered in ye presence of us

JOHN BOUGHAN, RALPH R SPEDE
JAMES BOUGHAN

Acknowledged by RALPH SPEED & right of Dower relinquished by ELIZA: his Wife in Essex County Court ye 11th day of September 1699 Test FRANCIS MERIWETHER, Cl Cur

p. KNOW ALL MEN by these presents that I ABIGALL PROSSER do give & make over
9 unto my Children, ANTHONY & JNO: PROSSER, and ye Child I now goe with, two

cowes & one calfe now in my possession with their female increase untill my sd Children shall come of ye age of Sixteen years, And then (severally they shall attain the age to have their part of ye aforesd Cow & female increase thereof) to them with their future increase forever & dureing ye minory of ye sd Children ye increase to be marked with a swallow forke on each eare, Also I give to my aforesd. Children one black Mare & fold by her side branced with with their future increase for ever In Witness whereof I have hereunto set my hand & seale this 8th of September 1699

Test JOHN PEATLE, ABIGALL A PROSSER
JNO: PROSSER

Acknowledged in Essex County Court ye 11th day of September 1699

pp. THIS INDENTURE made ye seventh day of September in ye yeare of our Lord God
9- One thousand six hundred ninety & nine Between JAMES BOUGHAN of ye Parish
10 of Farnham in ye County of Essex in ye Colony of Virga: Gent., of ye one part & THO: GREGSON of ye Parish of Sittenburne in ye same County, Gent., of ye other part, Witnesseth that in consideracon of three thousand pds. of good sound merchantable tobb: & caske unto mee ye sd JAMES BOUGHAN in hand truly paid, he ye sd JAMES BOUGHAN doth hereby grant unto ye sd THO: GREGSON his heirs & assignes forever all that parcell of land containing by estimacon Thirty acres being in ye County of Essex aforesd. formerly called RAPPA: County on a small branch or gutt that falled into OCCUPACON CREEKE and bounded as followeth that is to say Begining at a small red Oake on a point by a great Marsh it being ye corner tree of a tract of land formerly belonging to WM. HARPER but not belonging to THO: GREGSON and runing from ye sd corner tree North West along ye line of ye sd tract of land, from thence over the DEEP BRANCH to a marked red Oak by a DEEP BRANCH still keeping ye same Course along ye same line to a marked Pocikory that standeth on ye farther side of a Deep Branch that falleth into ye above sd small gutt of OCCUPACON CREEKE and then runing from ye sd Pocikery down ye branch into ye abovesd. small gutt or branch of OCCUPACON finally downe ye sd gutt or branch includeing all ye land between ye sd branch & ye aforemenconed line formerly of ye sd WM. HARPERs & now of ye sd THO: GREGSONs land, Together with all houses buildings barns tobacco houses orchards trees whatsoever belonging to ye sd land wch: said tract or parcell of land was granted & conveyed by LODOWICK ROWZEE, JNO: ROWZEE & EDWD. ROWZEE unto THO: CRIPPS by one Deed of Sale under their hands & seales bearing date ye Twenty sixth day of July Anno 1689 & by ye sd THO: CRIPPS assigned unto GEORGE PARKE deced by an Assignment thereof under his hand & seale endorsed on ye sd Deed of Sale & bearing date ye Twenty first day of Febry: 1695, And by ye last Will & Testamt. of ye sd GEO: PARKE given & devised unto ye sd JAMES BOUGHAN in fee simple & now is ye possession of ye sd THO: CRIPPS as Tenant unto ye sd JAMES BOUGHAN To have & to hold ye said tract of land to be sd THO: GREGSON his heirs & assignes from henceforth paying ye rents & services wch: shall hereafter become due unto our Sovereign Lord ye King And the sd JAMES BOUGHAN for himselfe his heirs doth promise that at all times forever after ye sd THO: GREGSON to enter into & enjoy ye sd tract of land without molestacon of ye sd JAMES BOUGHAN his heirs or assignes In Witness whereof ye parties first abovenamed have sett their hands & seales

Signed sealed & delivered in ye presence of us

THO: EDMONDSON, JAMES BOUGHAN
RICHD. COVINGTON,
FRANCIS GOULDMAN

Acknowledged in Essex County Court ye 11th day of 7ber: 1699 truely recorded

KNOW ALL MEN by these presents that I JAMES BOUGHAN am bound unto THO:

GREGSON of ye Parish of Cittenburne in ye County aforesd., Gent., in ye sum of Forty pds. of lawfull money of England to be paid dated ye seventh day of September One thousand six hundred ninety & nine

The Condicon of this obligacon is if ye above bound JAMES BOUGHAN his heirs or assignes shall truely perform all ye covenants menconed in one pair of Indentures bearing equall date with these presents between ye sd JAMES BOUGHAN of ye one part & ye abovenamed THOS: GREGSON of ye other part in all things, Then this obligacon to be void or else to remaine in full force

Signed sealed & delivered in presence of

THO: EDMONDSON, JAMES BOUGHAN
RICHD. COVINGTON
FRANCIS GOULDMAN

Acknowledged in Essex County Court ye 11th day of 7ber 1699 truely recorded

p. 10 TO ALL TO WHOM these presents shall come JNO. HAWKINS of ye Parish of Sittenburne in ye County of Essex within ye Colony of Virga: Gent., (only Son & heir of Major THOMAS HAWKINS late of ye same Parish & County, Gentl., deced) sendeth greeting Know yee that I ye sd JNO: HAWKINS as well for & in consideracon of ye good will love & affection wch: he hath & beareth unto his loveing Brother in Law, ROBT. MOSELEY, of ye Parish & County aforesd. Gent., as also for divers other good & valuable consideracons him thereunto moveing, he ye sd JNO: HAWKINS hath given unto ye said ROBT. MOSELEY all that tract or parcell of land containing by estimacon One hundred acres be ye same more or less scituate & being in ye Parish of Cittenburne & County of Essex aforesd., boundeth as followeth, that is to say, beginning at a marked white Oak standing at ye head of a branch issueing out of a Creek called ye FALCE CREEK and thence runing downe y esd branch to ye sd FALSE CREEK and thence by & nigh ye sd Creeke to Mr. LUCAS'S CREEK to a marked white Oake standing in ye Forke of a branch that falleth into ye sd LUCAS'S CREEK, & then North fifty seven degrees East to ye place where it first began together with all & singular its appurtenances & also ye Estate, right & demand wt:soever as well in equity as at Law of him ye sd JNO. HAWKINS to ye same wch: said parcell of land is part of ye tract of land whereon JNO. HAWKINS now liveth, To have & to hold ye sd tract of land unto ye sd ROBERT MOSELEY and ye heirs of his body lawfully to be begotten for ever, he ye sd ROBT. MOSELEY paying ye rents wch: shall from henceforth become due to our Sovereign Lord ye King and ye sd JNO: HAWKINS for himselfe and his heirs ye sd land with their appurtenances unto ye sd ROBT. MOSELEY and ye heirs of his body lawfully to be begotten for ever agt. him ye sd HAWKINS & all persons whatsoever claiming under him In Witness whereof he ye said JNO: HAWKINS hath hereunto set his hand & affixed his seale ye Ninth day of September Ano: Dom: 1699

Sealed & delivered in pr:sence of

JOHN PEATLE, JOHN HAWKINS
BARTHA: VAWTER

Acknowledged by JNO: HAWKINS & right of Dower relinquished by ELIZA: his Wife in Essex County Court ye 11th day of September 1699 & truely recorded FRANCIS MERIWETHER Cl Cur

Memorand: That it is agreed by & between ye parties within menconed that if ye sd ROBT. MOSELEY shall happen to dye without heirs of his body lawfully begotten then ye within menconed land to return to ye sd within named JNO. HAWKINS & his heirs forever anything in ye within menconed Deed to ye contrary notwithstanding Witness our hands ye daye & yeare within written

Witness JOHN PEATLE, ROBT. MOSELEY
BARTHA: VAWTER JOHN HAWKINS
Acknowledged in Essex County Court ye 11th day of September 1699 & truely recorded

p. 11 July ye 27th 1699. Then in Obedience to an Order of Court abearing date ye 10th day of Janry. 1698, we ye Subscribers being first sworne before Mr. THO: EDMONDSON have accordingly inventoried & appraised ye Estate of JOHN WOOD deced as was presented before us by WM. COX & FRANCES COX his Wife, & THO: WOOD, Exrs. of the Estate of JNO. WOOD as followeth:

By 20 ells of brown Line, 4 yds. of kersey, 3 yds. of Kersey, 1 Rogue, 1 card of buttons & parcell of remnants of Serge, 9 pewter dishes, six pewter plates, two basons, 1 chamber pott, 1 tankard & pint pott, 1 flagon, 1 pewter sauce pan, 1 pewter tumbler, 1 old tankard & parcell of old pewter, 3 porringers, a parcell of spoons, 1 stone mugg, 1 brass skillet, 1 pr. of wooll cards & parcell of old Tinn, 1 looking glass, 1 bottle & Ink horne, 1 comb; 1 pr. of marking irons, 1 pocket booke, 1 pr. sizors, 1 brass kettle, 1 old Bible, 6 wooden plates, 1 smoothing iron, 1 spining wheele, 1 straw coller & cart sadle, 3 hoes, a parcell of nailes, 2 truncks, 2 table & a quire of paper, 2 cross cutt saws & tent. saw, 2 files, 1 broad axe, 2 couchers, 1 old broad tray, 3 sider caskes, 1 bushell of lime, 2 corne baskets, 1 grindle stone, 4 sheep, 1 frying pann, 5 coes with calves at their sides, 1 barren cow, 3 two years old, 1 3 year old steer, 2 yearling steers, 25 lb. of feathers, 1 Callimanes Jacket, 1 pr. of small stiles, 2 old Sadle & bridle, 1 caster hatt, 1 felt hatt, 1 pair of worsted stockins, 1 wheele barrow, 1 old hoe, 1 old bed cord, 1 feather bed & furniture given to his Wife, 1 horse given to his Son, JOHN WOOD, 3 gunns given to his three Sons, 4 yds. of Serge given to his Mother, 1 Coat & breeches & 1 caster hatt, 1 feather bed & furniture given to his Son, JOHN, 1 bed ticken, 1 rogal, 1 pair of blanket given to his Son, THOMAS, by 1 Bible given to his Daughter, ELIZABETH, 1 bedstead, 1 small table cloth & six napkins, a parcell of Carpenters & Coopers old tooles, 1 branding iron & 1 razor, 2 yearlings ((Amounts of each item given but no total - Money)

FRANCIS BROWNE JOHN FARGESON
JA: FULLERTON JOHN HAILE

July ye 27th 1699
An Acct. of Debts due unto JNO. WOOD deced as followeth
Due from THOMAS FRANK, 350; due from JAMES QUARLES, 660, due from CHARLES BAGERLEY, 220; due from JOHN HAILE 060; due from Capt. RICHD. HAILE 040; due from JNO. BRASIER, 080; due from Widow SAVAGE, 100; due from AN CLARKE, 090; due from AN MOSS, 080; due from RICHD. TILER, 030; due from THOMAS BROWNE, 8-0; due from THOMAS BROWNE, 6-0; due from JOHN FARGESON 3-3-0; due from JONATHAN FISHER 1 pr. of mens shoes & 1-9; due from RICHD. BEALE 130; due from JOHN FARGESON 4 ells of linen; WILL COX Dr. 060; due from GEORGE TURNER, 040.

Sworne to by THO: WOOD & WM. COX & FRANCES his Wife in Essex County Court ye 11th day of 7ber: 1699 & truely recorded
Teste FRANCIS MERIWETHER, Cl Cur

FRANCIS BROWNE
JOHN FARGESON
JA: FULLERTON
JOHN HAILE

pp. 11-12 In Obedience to an Order of Essex Court dated ye 10th day of August 1699, we whose names are under written being a Jury summoned by ye Sheriff of ye sd County & sworne by Mr. RICHD. COVINGTON, one of his Majts. Justices, by ye Corts. order to inquire & lay out ye land in controversy between Mr. JOHN SMITH Plt. & Mr. THO: EDMONDSON Defendt., scituated in ye sd County according to ye ancient reputed bounds of ye Patent haveing regard to all evidences have upon due consideracon had to ye sd Plts. Patent which evidence as was produced by Plt. & Deft. according to ye order have been on ye land in Company of Mr. WM. GOUGH, Surveyor, & layd out ye same according to ye ancient boundes of ye sd Patent & do find ye Deft. a Trespasser within ye bounds of ye Plts. Patent to ye value of Ten pounds of tobo: Witness our hands & seales this seventh day of 7ber: 1699

JONATHAN FISHER	FRANCIS BROWNE	JA: FULLERTON
THOMAS ∩ MONDY	WM. TOMLIN	JOHN GATEWOOD
ROBERT 8 MILLS	ROBT. COLEMAN	RICHARD JONES
RICHARD R TAILER	THO: COVINGTON	JOHN HARPER

Truely recorded Test FRANCIS MERIWETHER, Cl Cur

p. Essex County ss) 7br: ye 5th. 1699
12 In Obedience to an Order of Essex County Court dated ye 10th day of Augt: 1699 in an accon between JOHN SMITH & ANN his Wife &c. Plts. & Mr. THO: EDMONDSON Defendt., with ye advice and direction of an Able Jury of ye sd County, I did survey & lay out a certaine tract of land formerly granted to Mr. JNO. COX, late of RAPPAHANNOCK County deced by Patent bearing date ye second day of Febr: 1653 according to ye sd Patent & ye Ancient known bounds hereof & do find that there is contained within ye bounds Twelve hundred & two acres of land begining at a Great Ellmn tree standing on bank of Rappa: River in COXES ISLAND on ye uper side of PUSCATTAWAY CREEKE mouth & runing up & by ye sd River side 450 poles crossing ye mouth of HOSKINS CREEKE, thence South West 320 poles into ye woods to two corner white Oakes in WHITE OAKE SWAMP, thence South East 130 poles to a great white Oake corner to a PATH side, thence So:west 75 poles into ye sd THO: EDMONDSONs Corne Feild, thence South 32 degrees East over severall small guts to an old marked Pine by PUSCATAWAY CREEKE side by ye mouth of JOHNSONS GUTT, thence down ye sd PUSCATAWAY CREEKE to ye begining tree dated 7br: ye 7th: 1699 finished

p WM. GOUGH, D. S. E.

Truely recorded test FRANCIS MERIWETHER, Cl Cur

p. Monday ye 21st of Novembr: 1698. Then attached in Obedience to ye contents of
12 ye other side that part of ye Crop in ye hands of Mr. SAML: SALLIS belonging to ye sd WALTER WHEATH (vizt) of tobacco some striped, some hanging & some packt, ye quantity no knowne till ye such time ye sd Cropp is fully finished & acct. given by ye sd SALLIS

p me REES EVANS

Truely recorded Test FRANCIS MERIWETHER, Cl Cur

pp. IN THE NAME of GOD Amen. I HENRY WILLIAMSON of ye County of Essex in ye
12- Colony of Virginia Gent. being sick & weak of body but of sounde perfect sence
13 & memory praise be to Almighty God for ye same do renounce all & singular any former Wills & Testamts. make this my last Will & Testamt. in manner & forme following vizt.

Impr. I bequeath my soul to God my Creatr: assured by believing that I shall receive full pardon & remission of all my sins & be saved by ye precious death & merits of my blessed Saviour & redeemer Christ Jesus and my body to ye Earth to be buried in such decent manner as to my Executrixs & Feoffees in Trust hereafter named shall think meet & convenient And all that worldly Estate as ye Lord in his mercy hath lent me after my just debts be fully satisfied, my will & meaning is ye same shall be imployed & bestowed as hereafter by this my Will is expressed

Item. I give & bequeath unto my Daughter, ELIZABETH, ten Negroes by name Scippio, Harrie, Tom, Betty ye Elder, Ginnie & her Daughter, Kate, Peter, Mingo, Franck & Sarah ye Younger and their increase to her & her heirs forever. I also give & bequeath unto my said Daughter, ELIZABETH, all that plantacon or devidend of land wherein I now live wch: sd land was bequeathed unto me by ye last Will & Testamt. of Capt. RICHD. LOES late of ye County of RAPPA. deced, with all ye houses orchards fences & appurtenances thereunto belonging unto her my said Daughter and ye heirs lawfully begotten of her body forever. Also I give & bequeath unto my said Daughter, ELIZABETH, all that plantacon and devidend of land whereon my MILL did stand qt: Four hundred and twenty acres with ye appurtenances & my right of entry of about One hundred acres of waste land adjoyning to ye said 420 acres wch: said land I have entered with Mr. EDWIN THACKER, Surveyr:, unto her my said Daughter & ye heirs lawfully begotten of her body for ever, but in case my said Daughter should die without issue lawfully begotten as aforesd., then I give & bequeath my said Plantacon & devidends of land with ye appurtenances unto my two other Daughters, KATHERINE & FRANCES, Surviveing to be equally divided between them & their heirs forever. I also give & bequeath unto my said Daughter, ELIZABETH, one third part of all my stock of Cattle, horses, mares, sheep, hoggs & one third part of all other my Estate not herein menconed or bequeathed unto her & her heirs for ever

Item. I give unto my Daughter, KATHERINE, & bequeath unto her ten Negroes by name Martin, Dick, Tom ye younger, Grace, Ann & her Son Ogany, Hanniball, Kate & Lettice & Charles & their encrease to her & her heirs fore ver. I also give & bequeath unto my Daughter, KATHERINE, halfe that plantacon & tract of land qt: seven hundred acres lying & being in MIDDLESEX County it being a Patent granted to Mr. ABRAHAM WEEKES ye moyety of ye sd land being by him & MILLICENT his Wife conveyed to me by Deed of Gift bearing date ye 30th day of June 1688 ye other halfe I purchased of Mr. FRANCIS WEEKES wth: ye houses orchards fences & other the appurtenances thereunto belonging. I do give unto my Daughter, KATHERINE, ye halfe of ye sd land to be equally divided & layed out for my said Daughter & her heirs lawfully begotten of her body for ever, but in case my said Daughter should die without issue lawfully begotten as aforesaid, then I give & bequeath my said plantation & her part of ye Dividend of land with ye appurtenances unto my other two Daughters Surviveing, ELIZ: & FRANCES, to be equally divided between them & their heirs for ever. I also give & bequeath unto my said Daughter, KATHERINE, One third part of all my stock of horses, mares, cattle, sheep, hoggs & one third part of all other my Estate not herein menconed or bequeathed unto her & her heirs for ever

Item. I give & bequeath unto my Daughter, FRANCES, ten Negroes by name Jack, Isaac, Mary & her Daughter Winnee, Jone, Joe & Betty, James & Phillip & Peggie with all their encrease unto her my said Daughter, FRANCES & her heirs for ever. I also give & bequeath unto my said Daughter, FRANCES, that Plantacon land I bought of Mr. FRANCIS WEEKES lying & being in ye County of MIDDLESEX with ye houses orchards fences & other ye appurtenances (being ye one moiety of a Devident of land formerly granted to Mr. ABRAHAM WEEKES) I do give unto my Daughter, FRANCES, & ye heirs lawfully begotten of her body for ever but in case my said Daughter should die without issue lawfully begotten as aforesaid, then I give my said Plantacon & land with ye appurtenances unto my other two Daughters Surviveing, ELIZABETH & KATHERINE, to be equally divided between them & their heirs forever. I likewise give & bequeath unto my said Daughter, FRANCES, one third part of all my Stock of horses, mares, cattle, sheep, hoggs, & one third part of all other my Estate not herein menconed or bequeathed unto her & her heirs for ever

Item. My will & desire is my INDIAN WOMAN named FRANCES being a Native Borne in this Country & her Mother also may be free if ye Law will permitt without transportacon, if not to remaine with ye rest of my Estate to be divided amonge my Children

Item. I give & bequeath unto my friends, Mr. EDWARD THOMAS, Mrs. LETTICE MOUNTAGUE & Mrs. ELIZABETH HILL & DANL. DOBYNS each of them a Ring of Thirty shillings price.

Item. I give & bequeath all other my Estate not herein menconed or bequeathed of what nature or kind soever unto my three Daughters above menconed & that ye same be inventoryed & put on record & equally divided between them & that they live together at my now dwelling house & their Negroes to be kept together upon my two plantacons & their cropps of tobo: annually sent for England & ye produce to remaine there until they shall attaine each of them respectively to full age by Law or Marryed, only such part as they shall have occasion for clothing & other necessaries, but in case my youngest Daughters should grow stubborn & not conformable to their elder Sister & Tutors then I shall leave it to ye discretion of my Feoffees in Trust to put them out to such Tutors as they shall think fit & convenient for their better education

Lastly, I do nominate ordaine & appoint my three Daughters, ELIZABETH, KATHERINE & FRANCES to be my sole & absolute Executrixes of this my last Will & Testamt. And the Honable Coll. RICHD. LEE Esqr., Capt. EDWARD THOMAS and Mr. SAML. PEACHEY & DANL. DOBYNS my Feoffees in Trust, willing & desireing them to pay all my just debts & legasies above menconed & to this my Will duely p:formed and this I deliver to ye world as my last Will & Testamt. Witness my hand & seale ye 30th of March 1699

Signed sealed & delivered in ye presence of

LEO: HILL, HENRY /V NICKSON, HENRY WILLIAMSON

DANL. DOBYNS, ANN A WHITEHORNE

Also tis my desire that ELLINORE DAVIS, ye Relict of THO: DAVIS have her dwelling on my back plantacon where there shee now is if remain a Widow, this done before signing & sealing

Proved in Essex County Court 11th day of September 1699 by ye Oathes of DANL. DOBYNS & LEO: HILL & truely recorded Test FRANCIS MERIWETHER, Cl Cur

p. 13 KNOW ALL MEN by these presents that wee THOS: MERIWETHER & ELIZABETH my Wife & DANL. WHITEHORNE & FRA: MERIWETHER of ye County of Essex are firmly bound unto ye Worpll. his Mats. Justices of ye Peace within the County of Essex in ye sum of Two thousand pds. Sterl. Witness our hands & seales this 11th day of 7ber: Ano: Dom: 1699

The Condicon of this obligacon is such that if the above named THO: MERIWETHER & ELIZ: his Wife, who at a Court held for this County the day & year above obtained a Probate of the last Will & Testament of HENRY WILLIAMSON deced shall doe at all times fullfill ye sd Will fully pay all such Legacies as therein expressed then this obligacon to be void or else to stand in full force

Signed & sealed in presence of

ROBT. MOSELEY

EDWARD GENTLEMAN

THO: MERIWETHER

ELIZ: MERIWETHER

DANL. WHITEHORNE

FRANCIS MERIWETHER

Truely recorded FRANCIS MERIWETHER, Cl Cur

p. 13 KNOW ALL MEN by these presents that I PETER RANSON of ye County of GLOCESTER Gent., have made ordained & constitute THOMAS PETTIS of ye County of KING & QUEEN my true & lawfull Attorney Generall for me to my use to aske sue for

receive from all persons whatsoever all & every such sums of money or tobacco as are now due & oweing or shall become due unto me by Bill bond accot. or any other waies or means and upon non payment thereof to sue imprison & prosecute and upon such suits to proceed to Judgmt. & upon paymt. of the same acquittances or other sufficient discharges in ye Law to make seale & deliver Attorney or Attorneys under him for ye purposes aforesaid to make and ye same at his pleasure to revoke & generally to do in & about ye premisses as fully as I my selfe might or could do if personally present. In Witness whereof I have hereunto set my hand this 11th day of 7ber: 1699
Signed sealed & delivered in presence of
JOHN PEATLE, PETER RANSONE
JAMES REEVES
Acknowledged in Essex County Court ye 11th day of 7ber: 1699 truely recorded

pp. 13-14 A true & perfect Inventory & appraisement of all & singular goods & chattells rights & credits of THOMAS GOULDMAN late of Essex County deced

At ye Home House

Negro Jupiter, Jack, Aggrig, Sam, Sambo, Betty, Kate, PATRICK MAGGARTT an Irish Boy, two old feather beds & furniture, one sett of Linsey curtains & vallens, one old chest, one ovill table, one chest of drawers, dozen of old leather chaires, pr. of Andirons, one warming pann, one brass kettle, iron potts & pott hooks, brass candlesticks, a slicer, a flesh fork, one copper pott & sauce pan; iron spitt, one Troopers Sadle Pistolls & Holsters, one looking glass, parcell of Woll, & pr. of Bellows, one gun, five pewter tankards, two doz: of pewter plates, two salts, five old pewter porringers, five pewter basons, eleven pewter dishes, one bason, two small saucers & three spoons, two old Chamber potts, one pewter dish. (Material: linen, sacking, coloured Fustian, German Dowlas, Narrow dowlas, Ozenbrigs, white Linen, printed Linen, Scotch Cloth, sheeting linen, holland, ticking, flannell, cotten, Napt. Cloth, kersey, lensey, Country grey, serge, color'd cotton, Dimothy, stuff printed linen, fine scotch cloth) a suit of cloathes, 2 table cloths & 12 napkins, 5 sheets & a pillow beer, 3 large Steers at 550 lbs. each, 3 smaller steers at 400 lbs. each; 2 small steers, 3 cows, 2 horses Total in pounds 42580

At ye Quarter by the River Side

To Bandie a Negro, Bess a Negro, one sorrell horse named Diamond, one gray horse, one black horse, one cow & calfe, 4 cowes, 3 three year old heifers, 2 two year old steers, 10 sheep, one pott & pott hooks 16240 1/2 Sum total: 58820 1/2

In Obedience to an Order of the Worshipful Court of Essex County bearing date ye 11th day of November 1698, wee whose names are subscribed being first sworne before Mr. ROBT. BROOKE did to ye best of our Judgmts. value & appraise ye within goods & chattells as it was exhibited by Mrs. DOROTHY GOULDMAN, Relict & Exex. of Mr. THOMAS GOULDMAN deced, In Witness whereof we have hereunto set our hands & seals this 3d of December 1699/8
Sworne before me JOHN DANGERFIELD JUNR.
RO: BROOKE SAMLL. THACKER
THOMAS HUCKLESCOTT

To a Servant sold to Mr. FRA: GOULDMAN 1500
To a Hogshead of Tob: due from WM. FOSSITT 0500
PETER RANSONE DOROTHY + RANSONE

Presented at a Court held for Essex County ye 11th day of 7ber: 1699 by PETER RANSONE & DOROTHY, his Wife, Exex. of THO: GOULDMAN deced, upon Oath as ye Inventory & appraismt. of ye sd deceds Estate (except such Estate as was willed by her former Husband RICHD. AWBREY in his Will to be delivered to his Children in Specie) & truely recorded

p. 14 Wee the Subscribers in obedience to an Order of Essex County Court bearing date ye 11th day of Augt. 1699 being first sworne before Mr. JAMES BOUGHAN this 24th day of Augt: have Inventoryed & appraised ye Estate of JNO. POWELL deced as was presented to us by THOMAS BURNETT & JANE his Wife, Admrs. of ye sd POWELLs Estate as follows:

To 3 cowes, 1 cow & calfe, heifer & steer, 1 feather bed & furniture, 1 flock bed rugg & blankett, a parcell of old chairs, 2 old chests, 1 trunk, a goon, 1 table, 6 trayes & 2 pailes, 1 chaney capp & salt seler, 1 old cattaile bed blanket, 1 cow hide, 4 old tubbs, 6 sider caske, one rimlet, 1 old cart & wheeles, a parcell of old iron, 4 bottles, a ladle, an old candlesticke, 1 looking glass, old towell, 1 frying pan & pott & pott hooks, 2 old books, 1 pewter tankard, one pewter pottenger, a parcell of pewter & ten pepper box, 6 pewter plates & pewter bason, 4 pewter dishes, 2 peper boxes, (value of items given but no total).

Sworne to before me JA: FULLERTON
JAMES BOUGHAN DANIEL BROWNE
JOHN FERGESON
THOMAS ᴖ WOOD

Sworne to in Essex County Court ye 12th day of 7ber: 1699 by THO: BURNETT & JANE his Wife, Admrs. of JNO: POWELL, deced, true recorded FRANCIS MERIWETHER, Cl Cur

p. 14 A true & perfect Inventory & appraismt. of ye Estate of SILVANUS TANDY deced taken & appraised by ye Subscribers this 8th day of 7ber: 1699

Imprs. 1 pr. of stilliards, pr. of pistoles & holsters, one long gunn, one brass morter & pestle, a parcell of old pewter & old tinn, a spitt & 2 iron pestelles one broken, 1 old frying pann, iron pott & pott hooks, old craked iron kettle, one old handsaw, one old adze, 3 iron wedges, one old sword, one old table & form, one old chest, one old grind stone, one five year old steer, one old couch & other old lumber, 2 old chairs & 2 old pailes, a parcell of old sider casks, a spade, grubing hoe & one old sifter, a parcell of lumber, ten pds. of feathers, one old rugg & blankets (items valued, not totalled)

In Obedience to an Order of ye Worpll. Court of Essex, wee ye Subscribers did value & appraise ye above Estate as it was exhibited to us by JOHN PARKER & MARTHA his Wife, & have hereunto sett our hands & seales ye 9th day of 7ber: 1699

EDMUND PAGETT
THO: HUCKLESCOTT
SAML. THACKER

7ber: ye 8th: 1699 this day in Obedience to ye last Courts Order ye appraisers were by me Sworne FRANCIS GOULDMAN

Sworne to in Essex County Court ye 12th day of 7ber: 1699 by JOHN PARKER truely recorded

p. 14 TO ALL CHRISTIAN PEOPLE to whom this present writing shall come I FRANCIS GIBSON of Sittingborne Parish in Essex County send greeting in our Lord God everlasting this Tenth day of October in ye yar 1699. Now Know yee that I the said FRANCIS GIBSON for & in consideracon of Two thousand six hundred pounds of tobacco in hand paid to me by HENRY LONG of ye sd Parish & County have granted unto him ye sd HENRY LONG his heirs one tract of land containing One hundred & eleven acres more or less being ye land wch: my Father, WM. GIBSON, bought of RICHD. WEST by Deed dated ye 29th: of March 1666 begining & bounded as by ye said Deed will appear unto ye said HENRY LONG his heirs & assignes forever with all its rights & appurtenances together with all houses edifices gardens orchards woods To have & to hold unto ye said HENRY LONG his heirs & assignes And I ye sd FRANCIS for himselfe his

heirs will warrant & for ever defend by these presents from ye claimes of any persons wt:soever And that it is clear of all other grants titles or incumbrances; I ye sd FRANCIS do promise that ye sd HEN: LONG his heirs & assignes shall peaceably hold ye sd land forever In Witness whereof I ye sd FRANCIS GIBSON have set my hand & seale
Signed & delivered in presence of

JNO: BATTAILE, FRAN: F GIBSON
MARY J WARD
ROBT. A ANJEON

Acknowledged in Essex County Court ye 10th day of November 1699 truely recorded

p. 15 THIS INDENTURE made ye 5th day of October in ye year of our Lord God One thousand six hundred ninety & nine Between GILES CURTIS of ye County of MIDDLESEX, Planter, of ye one part & WILLIAM HUDSON of ye County of Essex, Planter, of ye other part. Witnesseth that ye said GILES CURTIS for a valuable sum to be paid on demand hath sold unto ye sd WM: HUDSON his heirs & assignes Two hundred acres of land being prt of a parcell of land formerly Mr. NICHOLAS COCKE bounded on ye land of Mr. COCKE & on ye land of HENRY WOODNOT and runing along ye DRAGON SWAMP side, To have & to hold all & every the hereby sold premisses with their appurtenances to him ye said WILLIAM HUDSON his heirs & assignes for ever together with all woods water fishing fowling hawking & all other rights to ye same belonging and ye said GILES CURTIS doth for himselfe grant & agree that ye sd premisses free & clear from all other sales & incumbrances And that he ye sd WM. HUDSON his heirs or assignes shall peaceably hold & enjoy ye sd premisses without ye trouble or denial of him ye sd GILES CURTIS his heirs or any claiming under him In Witness whereof ye sd GILES MARTIN hath hereunto set my hand & seale ye day & year first above written
Signed sealed & delivered in ye presence of

CHRISTOPHER BERNARD, GILES S CURTIS
RICE CURTIS

RICE CURTIS by vertue of a Power of Attorney from GILES CURTIS acknowledged this Deed of Sale in Essex County Court ye 10th day of November 1699

KNOW ALL MEN by these presents that I GILES CURTIS of ye County of MIDDLESEX doth impower & demise my well beloved Son, RICE CURTIS, to be my true good & lawfull Attorney with warranty to acknowledge two hundred acres of land in ye County of Essex as by Deed will appear as Witness my hand & seale ye fourth of November 1699
Test JOHN COGLON, I GILES G CURTIS
RICE CURTIS

Prov'd in Essex County Court ye 10th day of November 1699 by ye oathes of ye Witnesses hereto truely recorded Test FRANCIS MERIWETHER, Cl Cur

p. 15 TO ALL &c. Whereas &c. Now Know yee that I ye sd Sr. WM. BERKELEY Knt. &c. do with ye consent of ye Councill of State accordingly give & grant unto JNO. PROSSER Four thousand Eight hundred ninety two acres of land in ye Freshes of Rappa. above NANZATICON next ye land of Mr. JNO: PAYNE on ye So: side of ye River begining at a marked Oake at or by the River side that parts him & Mr. JNO. PAINE & runing down ye River over a Creeke called ye GOULDEN VALE to a white Oake ye corner of JNO. GILLETTs land deced, So: East 400 poles thence into the woods with GILLETTs line So. West 330 pches. to a marked stake within sight of certaine hills, thence So. East 300 poles on ye back line of GILLETTs, thence East 10 pches., thence So. East on a back line of land formerly CLEMENT HORBIRTs to a Pokhicory upon PEWMANSON CREEK 150 pches. thence So. West 480 pches. to a white Oake hanging over ye maine branch of PEWMAN-

SONS CREEKE, thence No. West 320 pches. to a PATH, thence So. West 240 pches. to a marked Oak, thence North West 900 poles, thence North East to ye line of Mr. JNO. PAINE near ye head of MAZAPIN SWAMP 452 pches., thence North East by ye So. East 352 perches with PAYNEs line, thence East No. East 10 degrees & 1/2 Northerly 420 pches, thence Easterly to ye place began near ye River; To have & to hold &c. ye sd being due unto ye sd JNO: PROSSER by & for ye transportacon of Ninety persons into this Colony To have & to hold &c. yeilding & paying &c. provided &c. Dated ye 8th day of 8ber 1665
Recordatr 13th 8br: 1665 WILLIAM BERKELEY
PHILL: LUDWELL, Cl Off:
Truely recorded according to an Ordr. of Essex County Court ye 10th day of 9ber 1699

p. 15 KNOW ALL MEN by these presents that I RICHD. BRIDGE of Leverpool in ye County of Lancastr:, Merchant, & now Supra Cargoe of ye Shipp, *LAMB of LEEVERPOOL,* (whereof Capt. JNO. THOMAS is now Commandr) have made PAUL MICOU of Essex County in Virga: Agent & Supra Cargoe for PETER ATHERTON SENR. of LEEVERPOOL, Merchant, & who wlse are or may be concerned this present Voyage in ye sd Shipp my true & lawfull Attorney for me & to ye use of PETER ATHERTON & COMPA. to aske demand sums of mony tobaccos as are due unto me for goods sold by me for acct. of ye sd PETER ATHERTON and COMPA., And in case of non payment I do impower my sd Attorney to arrest in prison implead & sue to Judgmt. & execution, I do impower my said Attorney to give acquittance or any other legall discharges as fully as myselfe might or could do were I personally present confirming whatsoever my said Attorney shall legally do In Witness whereof I have sett my hand & seale ye Twenty ninth day of March 1699
Sealed & delivered in ye presence of
ARGOL BLACKSTAN RICHD. BRIDGE
JOHN STODGILL
Prov'd in Essex County Court by ye Oathes of ye witnesses hereto ye 10th day of 9ber: 1699

pp. 15-16 THIS INDENTURE made this Seventeenth day of October in ye Eleaventh yeare of ye Reign of our dread Soveraigne William by ye grace of God King of England Scotland france and Ireland &c. Betweene RICHARD COVINGTON of South Farnham Parish and County of Essex, Gent., and ANN his Wife on ye one part and MARY ST. JOHNS of ye aforesd. Pish. and County, Widow, on ye other part; Wittnesseth that ye said RICHARD COVINGTON for and in consideration of ye sum of Three thousand pounds of sweet scented tobacco and cask to him paid hath sold unto ye sd MARY ST. JOHNS her heirs and assignes forever a certaine parcell of land belonging to ye BEST LAND DEVIDENT beinge in ye foresd. Parish and County adjoyning to ye land of MARY ST. JOHNS bounding as followeth, Begining on ye North side of ye DRAGON SWAMP at a corner tree of ye sd MARY ST. JOHNS land and so up ye said Maine Swamp to ye mouth of a branch called ye WHITE OAKE BRANCH and so up ye sd branch to a small slash issueing out of ye said branch and so up ye sd slash by marked trees to a PATH that goeth from MARY ST. JOHNS to THOMAS HAWERTONs and so downe ye sd PATH to ye land of ye said MARY ST. JOHNS containeing Fifty acres of land more or less togather with all wayes & waters commodities and appurtenances belonging And all ye right and Interest which he the said RICHARD COVINGTON now hath, also all Deeds Patents and writings concerning ye same to ye only proper use and behoof of ye sd MARY ST. JOHNS her heires and assignes for ever And ye sd. RICHARD COVINGTON for himselfe his heirs doth promise that he hath good right to sell & convey the sd premisses and that ye same shall remaine unto her ye sd MARY ST. JOHNS her heirs & assignes forever free from all former grants and that he will warrant and for ever defend ye sd MARY ST. JOHNS her heirs in the quiet free and peaceable enjoyment of ye above grant against him his heirs & assigns as against all other persons lawfully claimeing under him And Lastly, that he ye sd RICHARD COVINGTON and ANN his Wife shall make acknowledgement of these presents and her right of Dower in open Court held for Essex County when thereunto required In wittness whereof the sd RICHARD COVINGTON and ANN his Wife hath sett their hands & seales

Signed sealed & delivered in ye presents of us

ARTHUR: A HODGES, RICHARD COVINGTON
SAMLL. COATES ANN COVINGTON

p. 16 TO ALL CHRISTIAN PEOPLE to whom these presence shall come I MARY ST. JOHNS of Southfarnham Parish in ye County of Essex, Widow, send greeting in our Lord God everlasting. Know ye that I MARY ST. JOHNS for ye tendr: love good will & affection wch: I have & bear unto my two dear & loveing Sons, THO: ST. JOHNS & WM: ST. JOHNS of Southfarnham Parish & County of Essex and for divers other good causes me hereunto moving hath granted & by these presents do give unto my two deare & loveinge Sons, THO: ST. JOHNS & WM. ST. JOHNS their heirs and assignes forever all ye land wch: I now live upon wch: my late Husband, THO: ST. JOHNS since deced, formerly bought of Coll: WM. CLAIBOURNE scituate and being in Southfarnham Parish in ye aforesd. County as also that tract & parcell of land wch: ye sd MARY ST. JOHNS lately bought of Mr. RICHARD COVINGTON all wch: sd plantation & land doth containe by estimation Two hundred & fifty acres more or less togather with all wayes and profitts thereunto belonging, ye sd plantacon & land to be equally divided betwixt ye sd THO: ST. JOHNS & WM. ST. JOHNS To have and to hold all and singular ye sd Plantacon wth: ye appurtenances unto them their heirs and assignes forever upon this Provison and Reservation: yt: the sd MARY ST. JOHNS & JNO: BILLINGTON shall occupy possess enjoy ye sd plantation & land dureing their naturall lives or the longest Survivor of them two without the molestation or disturbance of ye sd THO: ST. JOHNS & WM. ST. JOHNS their heirs or assignes or any other p:son whatsoever through their meanes and that ye sd THO: ST. JOHNS shall enjoye one halfe of ye Orchard belonging to ye sd Plantation after ye sd MARY ST. JOHNS decease And further yt: my Daughter, ELIZ: COOPER, ye now Wife of WM. COOPER, shall have free Liberty her & her husband dureing her naturall life to remaine abide & be upon ye sd plantation where they are now leased dureing her naturall life but if in case ye Surviver be her sd Husband, WM. COOPER, to have ye same privitie upon ye sd Plantation during his naturall life according to a Lease Instrumt. or writeing signed sealed & delivered unto ye sd WM. COOPER & his Wife by THO: ST. JOHNS my late Husband since deced & further yt: my two Sons, THO: ST. JOHNS & WM. ST. JOHNS shall have free privilidge & liberty to seat upon ye land upon any part or parcell

thereof if they cove:t when each of them shall attaine to ye age of Eighteene yeares provided it be not to ye hinderance disturbance or damage of me ye sd MARY ST. JOHNS & JNO: BILLINGTON In Witness whereof I have hereunto set my hand & seale this 9th day of Nobr: in ye Eleventh yeare of ye Reign of our Soveraigne Lord Wm. ye Third King of England & in ye yeare of our Lord God 1699
Signed sealed and delivered in ye presence of
EDWARD DANELANE MARY H ST. JOHNS her marke
JNO. PROSSER
Acknowledged in Essex County Court ye 10th day of 9ber 1699 and truely recorded

pp. 16-17 IN YE NAME OF GOD Amen I THO: HINES of Essex County being sicke & weake in body but of perfict sence and memory thankes be to God doe make this my last Will & Testamt. in manner as follows. Imprimi: I bequeath my Soule to Almighty God who gave itt mee in sure and certaine hopes of salvation through ye merritts of my blessed Saviour & Redeemer Jesus Christ and my body to ye Earth to be buried in such Christian like manner as my Deare Wife shall see fitt

Item. I give and bequeath unto my Son, THO: HINES one hundred & fifty acres of land dureing ye terme of his naturall life and after his decease I doe will and bequeath ye sd hundred & fifty acres of land to be equally divided betweene my two Sons, HENRY and JON: HINES to them and theire heires forever ye sd land lying on ye West side of WHITE MARSH from my dweling house

Item. I give unto my Sone, THO: HINES, one man Servt., five yeares to serve and one feather bed and furniture, two Milch cows and calves, one young mare that came of my Sorrell Mare last & one gray Ston Horse about three years old, one iron pott, one pewter dish, two Milke trayes & halfe dozen spoons, my sword and pistall and all my Coopers tools

Item. I give & bequeath unto my Son, THO: HINES two breeding sows, two barrows of two yeares old and all my wearing cloathes all ye above sd (except ye Land) I give unto my sd THO: HINES to him and his heires forever

Item. It is my will and desire that my sd Son, THO: HINES, doe stay wth: my Wife and assist to finish this present cropp and when so don I do will and appoint unto my sd Son, THO: HINES, one equal share of ye sd Cropp both Indian Corne & tobacco

Item. I give unto my Son, THO:, one large new chest & doe hereby make him my sd Son: THO: of full age

Item. I give and bequeath unto my two Sons, HENRY HINES and JON: HINES, all that parcell of land I now dwell on to be equally divided betweene them and their heires for ever. After my Wifes decease, I doe give and bequeath all ye rest of my Estate, cattle, horses, mares, sheep, hoggs and all my household goods to be equally divided betweene my dear Wife, HANNAH HINES, and my Five Children begotten of her to them and their heirs fore ever

Item. I doe appoint my dearely and well beloved Wife, HANNAH, to be my whole and sole Executrix of this my last Will and Testamt.

Item. I nominate and appoynt my two good friends, DANLL. DOBYNS and Mr. DANLL. WHITEHORNE to be my feoffees in Trust of ye same

In Wittness hereof I have put my hand and fixed my seale this 16th: day of 7ber: 1699
Test DANLL. DOBYNS, THOMAS H HINES
WM. W HUDSON, THOMAS BEATSON
Proved by ye oathes of ye Wittnesses hereto in Essex County Court ye 10th day of November 1699 & truely recorded. Test FRANCIS MERIWETHTER, Cl Cur

p. 17 KNOW ALL MEN by these presents that we HANNAH HINES, HENRY PICKETT, HENRY WOODNETT of ye County of Essex are firmly bound unto his Majties. Justices of ye peace for ye sd County of Essex in ye sum of Forty thousand pounds of tobacco & caske we bind ourselves this 10th day of 9:ber Anno Dom: 1699

The Condition of this obligation is that if HANNAH HINES who at Court held for Essex County ye day and yeare abovesd: obtained a Probate of ye last Will of THO: HINES deced, shall at all times hereafter fulfill ye sd: Will and satisfie all such Legatees as therein are expressed and do whatsoever ye Law enjoynes in such cases then ye above obligation to be void otherwise to remaine of full force

Signed sealed & delivered in presents of us

PHILL: PARR, HANNAH H HINES
ROBT. COLEMAN HENRY H PICKET
HENRY R WOODNUT

Truely recorded Test FRANCIS MERIWETHER, cl Cur

p. 17 KNOW ALL MEN by these presents that we JON: CAMELL and SARAH CAMELL his Wife of ye Parrish of South farnham in ye County of Essex for ye sum of Two thousand and seven hundred pounds of lawfull tobaccoe to us in hand paid by HENRY PICKETT of ye said Parrish & County hath sold unto ye sd HENRY PICKETT his heires & assignes forever One hundred acres of land scituate and being in ye said Parrish of Farnham and County of Essex back in ye woods and on ye branches of PASCATACON CREEK it being part and parcell of a tract of land formerly belonging to JOHN KILLMAN, Father of ye said SARRAH CAMELL, and descending by the death of ye said JOHN KILLMAN unto his Son, GEORGE KILLMAN, Brother of ye said SARAH CAMELL, and by the death of the said GEORGE KILLMAN, unto ye sd SARAH CAMELL To have and to hold ye said One hundred acres of land begining at a white Oake corner tree to ye land of JON: MITCHALL and runing thence South East by ye said MITCHALLs land to a marked white Oake standing by a branch called ye GREEN SWAMP, thence West South West down ye said Swamp to a marked white Oke by the said Swamp, thence North West downe by the Swamp called by BEVERDAM SWAMP to a marked white Oke, thence East North East into the woods to the first mentioned Corner tree to him ye said HENRY PICKETT ye said One hundred acres of land wth: all its rights & appurtenances belonging To have use & enjoy and to his heirs & assignes forever And we ye said JON: CAMELL & SARAH CAMELL for our selves our heires ye said land sold unto ye sd HENRY PICKETT and his heires forever against us the sd JON: CAMELL and SARAH CAMELL our heires and assignes and all other persons under them In Witness of all and every the above recited premisses and all ye articles & clauses and in confirmation of them and every of them, we the sd JON: CAMELL and SARAH CAMELL doe hereunto put our hands and seales this 20th day of January 1696

Sealed & delivered in pr:sence of us

THO: PARKER SENR. JON: I CAMELL
WILLIAM WALL, SARAH IY CAMELL
JOHN G GATEWOOD,
SARAH PICKETT

Acknowledged in Essex County Court ye 10th day of May 1697 by the above named JON: CAMELL and SARAH his Wife, (ye sd SARAH being privately examined according to Law) & truely recorded

BE IT KNOWN unto all men to home it may concerne that I HENRY PICKETT and SARY PICKETT his Wife of ye County of Essex do asure over all our rites and tytells of this within menchoned convaiance unto THO: HINES JUNOR. from me and my ares to

THO: HINES and his ares for ever, To have and to hould for ever, I ye sd HENERY PICKETT douth wirront ye sale of this land from all parsons or parson whatsoever that shall rase any justly and likewise I afarme over to the said THO: all ye full preveledges that is within menchoned as formly as it is to me afarmed as wittness my hand & seale this 9th day of November 1699

THO: BOATSON HENRY H PICKET
HANAH H HINDES

Acknowledged ye right of Dower relinquished in ye Essex County Court ye 10th day of November 1699 freely Truely recorded Test FRANCIS MERIWETHER, Cl Cur

pp. 18-19 THIS INDENTURE made ye Seaventh day of May in ye yeare of or: Lord God One thousand six hundred Ninety & eight between RICHARD COOPER of ye Parrish of South farnham in ye County of Essex of ye one part and SAMLL. GRISSELL of KINGSTONE Parish in GLOSTER County of ye other part Witnesseth that whereas ye said RICHARD COOPER by Indenture bearing date ye Sixth day of May in ye yeare of or: Lord One thousand six hundred Ninty & eight for ye consideracon therein expressed did sall unto ye sd DANLL. GRISSELL Eighty acres of land being in ye above Pish. of South farnham & County of Essex & adjoyning to ye sd RICHD. COOPER plantation & lying between ye said Plantation & ye land of EVEN DAVIS and begining to be measured neare yee plantation of ARTHUR HODGES at a marked Spanish Oake corner tree to EVEN DAVIS & runeth South West to a white Oke, thence South West to a Hicory, thence South to a stoopinge red Oack by ye MILL PATH & thence South by West to five marked red Oacks by a Pine & thence West to a marked pokhicroy & thence North West to ye first Station togeather with all ye woods & underwoods houses fencings orchards profitts to ye sd Eighty acres of land belonging. NOW THIS INDENTURE Witnesseth that ye sd RICHD. COOPER for ye sume of Twelve hundred pounds of good sweet scented tobacco & cask to him by ye said SAMLL. GRISSELL payd whereof he doth grant unto ye said SAMLL. GRISSELL in his actuall possession now being by vertue of ye sd recited Indenture of bargaine & sale made to him for a Yeare & of ye Statute and to his heires & assignes ye aforesd. land and all ye rights & demands whatsoever of ye sd RICHD. COOPER togeather with all his rights wt:soever as is before expressed To have & injoy ye sd Eighty acres of land wthout any molestacon of ye sd RICHD. COOPER his heires or assignes or any other p:sons whatsoever claiming ye same that he ye sd RICHD: COOPER & ANN his Wife will p:sonally appear at ye next Court held for ye County of Essex & by this Instrumt. of writing yeild up & acknowledge all their right of ye above pr:misses unto ye sd SAMLL. GRISSELL his heires & assignes for ever In Witness whereof ye sd RICHD. COOPER & ANN his Wife hath hereto sett their hands & seales

Signed sealed & delivered in pr:sence of us

THOMAS T WILLIAMS, RICHD: + COOPER
WM: M WILLIAMS ANN (I) COOPER

Acknowledged and right of Dower relinquished in Essex County Court ye 10th day of November 1699 and truely recorded. Test FRANCIS MERIWETHER, Cl Cur

KNOW ALL MEN by these pr:sents yt: I RICHD. COOPER of ye Pish. of South farnham in ye County of Essex am bound unto SAMLL. GRISSELL of KINGSTONE Pish. in GLOSTR: County in ye full sume of Two thousand pounds of good sweet scented tobacco & caske Witness signed with my hand dated ye seaveth day of May in ye yeare of or: Lord God One thousand six hundred Ninty & eight

The condicon of this pr:sent obligacon is that whereas ye above bounden RICHD. COOPER hath by a Deed of Lease dated ye Seaventh day of this Instant moneth for a valuable consideracon therein menconed sold unto ye above named SAMLL. GRISSELL

Eighty acres of land and by a Deed of Release dated 10th wth: these presents for ye valuable consideracon therein recited hath granted and confirmed unto ye said SAMLL. GRISSELL his heirs & assignes for ever ye sd Eighty acres of land, If therefore ye above named SAMLL. GRISSELL shall at all tymes forever from henceforth quietly hold ye sd land clearly discharged from all trouble or incumbrances made by ye above bound RICHD. COOPER his heirs or any other p:sons and also execute all things needfull & necessary for ye secureing ye tytle & Estate of ye sd Eighty acres according to ye intent of ye abovesd. Deeds, Then this pr:sent obligacon to be voyd or else to stand in full force
Signed sealed & delivered in ye pr:sence of us

THO: WILLIAMS, RICHD: COOPER
WM: WILLIAMS
PHILL: PARR

Acknowledged in Essex County Court ye 10th day of November 1699 & truely recorded

pp. IN YE NAME OF GOD Amen ye Second day of June 1698 I LODWICK ROWZEE being
19- sick & weak in body but of sound & perfect memory praysed be giveing to God
20 for ye same knowing ye Oncertainty of this life on Earth and being desirous to settle things in order doe make this my last Will and Testament in manner & forme following, that is to say, first and principall I commend my Soul to Almighty God my Creator assuredly beleaving that shall receive full pardon & free remission of all my sins and be saved by ye precious death & merrits of my sd Redeemer Christ Jesus my bodie to ye Earth from whence itt was taken to be buried in such descent Christian manner as to my Execrs. hereafter named shall be thought fitt and convenient as touching my worldly Estate as ye Lord in mercy hath lent me, my will & meaning is ye same shall be imployed as hereafter by this my will is expressed

First, I doe revoke and renounce frutrate & make voide all Wills by me formerlie made & declared and appoint this my last Will & Testament. First & foremost that all debts due from me to any man bee satisfied.

Item My will is that ye Seat of Land given to me & my Brother by our Father, Mr. EDWARD ROWZEE, if my Brother, EDWARD ROWZEE, shall have a male Child lawfully begottin of his one bodie, my will is that he have ye third part of my land saving & excepting One hundred acers giveing by my Brother, JOHN ROWZEE deced, to our Cozen, ELIZABETH NORTH & her heires for ever Ye other third part of itt shall please God that my Sistr: SARAH NORTH, have a male Child lawfully begotten of her bodie

Item My will is wth ye same exception of aforenamed that then my will be he shall have ye other third part him and his heirs forever

Item My will is that if my Sistr: ELIZABETH shall have a male Child lawfully begotten of her own bodie, he shall have ye other third part for him & his heires forever but now if itt shall soe please God to happen to appear to ye full age of one & twentie yeares that then my will is my Brother, EDWD., shall have hold & injoy all ye sd Devident of land duringe his naturall life now if itt shall please God that none of those heires afore named shall appeare to full age afore named then my will is that it shall run & be entailed upon my Cozen, RALPH ROWZEE JUNIOR & my Cozen, EDWARD ROWZEE JUNIOR that itt shall run in theire use and behalfe and theire heires for ever, but if itt please God my Brother, EDWARD, shall marry a Wife and should have a female Child lawfully begotten of his bodie by his bethrothed Wife that then my will is that then tht female Child shall have hold and enjoy all ye aforesd. land before my two Cozens, RALPH & EDWARD.

Item My will is that Mr. GEORGE PLEY shall have free previlige during his naturall life occuping and making use of as much of ye ground about ye houses as he shall have occation for himselfe & one more for plant

Item I give unto my loveing friend, WM. HARPER, my new chest
Item My will is that SAMLL. CARTER have ye privelige for four yeares of wt. ground he can make use of
Item I give unto my Brother, EDWARD, my bed & furniture
Item I give unto my Sister, SARAH, my new bed & furniture
Item I give unto my Brother, EDWD., my flock bed
Item My will is that my Neighbour, ELLIONER PARKER & her Children may have ye previlige of ye Orchard for eating Apples during her life without molestation
Item I give unto my Brother, EDWD. ROWZEE, all my moveables and immoveables within & without dores. My desire is that JON: SURREL: may have ye privilige of beatinge Sixty gallans of Sider yearlie for ye terme of fore yeares in case ye Orchard hitts
I doe appoint my loveing Brother, Mr. EDWD. ROWZEE my Sole Executr: of this my last Will & Testament In Witness hereof I have hereunto sett my hand & seale ye day & yeare above mentioned
Sealed & delivered in pr:sents of us
WM. HARPER, LODWICK ROWZEE
SAMLL. CARTER
Proved by ye Oath of WM. HARPER in Essex County Court ye 10th day of June 1699 & by ye Oath of SAMLL. CARTER ye 10th day of November following & truely recorded

KNOW ALL MEN by these pr:sents that we EDWARD ROWZEE and THOMAS GREGSON of ye County of Essex are firmly bound unto his Majties: Justices of ye peace for ye sd County of Essex in ye sum of Ten thousand pounds of tobacco and caske Witness our hands & seales this 10th day of 9br: Anno Dom. 1699.
The Condicon of this obligacon is that if EDWARD ROWZEE who at a Court held for ye abovesd. County of Essex ye day & date aforesd. obtaind. a probate of ye last Will of LODODWICK ROWZEE deced, do at all times hereafter fullfull & fully pay all such Legatees as are expressed & perform all ye Law enjoynes in such cases, Then ye above obligacon to be void otherwise to remain in full force
Signed sealed & delivered in pr:sents of us
ROBT. MOSELEY, EDWARD ROWZEE
EDWARD GOULDMAN THO: GREGSON
1699 Truely recorded FRANCIS MERIWETHER, Cl Cur

p. May ye 24th 1698. IN YE NAME OF GOD Amen, I JON: ROWZEE of Essex County
20 being sick & weake of body but of perfict cence & memory praise be given to God for ye same & knowing ye uncertaine Estate of this life hereon Earth & being desirous to settle things in order do make this my last Will & Testament in manner & forme following, that is to say, first & principally I commend my Soule to God allmighty my Creator who gave it & my body to ye Earth from whence it was taken assuredly beleveing that I shall receive full pardon for my Sinns & be saved by ye presious death & merrits of my blessed Savour & redeemer Christ Jesus Amen.
Item I give unto my loveing Coussen, ELIZABETH NORTH, One hundred acers of land begining at a place called YOUNG THO: PARKERS FOLLY ye bounds to be along ye Norwest side of a Swamp called ye BACK SWAMP & soe for length to ye Maine Creeke to her & her heirs lawfully begotten for ever, But if it should please God yt: my coussen, ELIZABETH, should depart this life before she hath any lawfull issue borne that then Item. my will is yt: my loveing Coussen, JANE NORTH, shall have & injoy ye aforesd land shee & her heires lawfully begotten of her one body for ever
Item My will is yt: ye aforesd. hundred acres of land shall bee in ye custidy & ocipation of my loveing Brother, LODOWICK ROWZEE.

Item I give my Loveing Sister, SARAH NORTH, teen plates & a saltseler;
Item I give unto my loveing Brother, EDWARD ROWZEE, what sheepe I have
Item I give unto my loveing Brother, ED: ROWZEE, one Cow called Bournin
Item I give unto my loveing Brother, LODOWICK ROWZEE, three cowes & three steares & a bull them & their increas to him and his heires for ever
Item I give unto my loveing Brother, LODOWICK ROWZEE two horses the one called Snip the other called Shavour
Item I give unto my lov: Brother, ED: ROWZEE, 10 yards & one halfe of broad cloath, buttons, silk & lineing to it
Item My will is that my lovo: Brother, LODOWICK ROWZEE & my loveing Brother, EDWARD ROWZEE be & remaine my soale Exercrs. of this my last Will and Testament
Signed sealed & published in the pr:sence of

WM. HARPER, JOHN I ROWZEE
SAMLL. CARTER

Proved by ye Oath of WM. HARPER in Essex County Court ye 10th day of June 1699 & by ye Oath of SAMUEL CARTER ye 10th of November following and truely recorded

KNOW ALL MEN by these pr:sents that we EDWD. ROWZEE & THO: GREGSON of ye County of Essex are firmly bound unto his Majties. Justices of ye peace for ye said County in ye sum of Ten thousand pounds of tobacco & caske Witness our hands & seales this 10th: day of 9ber: 1699

The Condition of this obligation is that if ye above bound ED: ROWZEE who at a Court held for Essex County ye day & yeare abovesd. obtained a Probat of ye Last Will of JON: ROWZEE deced, shall at all times herefter fullfill ye sd Will, fully pay & satisfie all such Legacies as are expressed and doe all & wt:soever ye Law injoynes in such cases, Then ye above obligation to be void otherwayes remaine in full force
Signed Sealed & Delivered in ye pr:sence of

ROBT. MOSELEY, EDWARD ROWZEE
EDWARD GOULDMAN THO: GREGSON

Truely recorded Test FRANCIS MERIWETHER, Cl Cur

pp. 20-21 IN YE NAME OF GOD Amen the Twenty fifth day of Maye in ye yeare of our Lord God 1699, I SOLOMAN HARPR: of Essex County, Planter, being sick & weak in body but of perfect mind & memory thanks be given to God therefore calling to mind ye mortality of my body and knowing that it is appointed for all men once to die do make & ordain this my last Will & Testament that is to say principally & first of all I give & recommend my Soul into the hands of him yt: gave it & for my body I commend it to ye Earth to be buried in a Xtian. like & decent manner at ye discretion of my Exers. nothing doubting but at ye generall Resurrection I shall receive ye same again by ye Mighty Power of God And as touching such worldly Estate wherewith it hath pleased God to bless me with in this life, I give devise & dispose of the same in ye following manner & form

Imprimis I give & bequeath to my Brothr:, THOMAS HARPR:, & to WM: HARPR: ye Eldest Son of my Brothr: JNO: HARPR:, all & singular part & parcell of land yt: by right doth justly belong to me to be equally devided betwixt ye sd THO: HARPR: & WM: HARPR: & ye sd land to be reserved & kept in my Brothr: JNO: HARPERs, possession till they be of age & if ye sd THO: HARPER or WM. HARPER dye wthout heire Legitimate then to descend to the next legall heirs of yt: race or Consanquinty of ye sd HARPRs. Nevr: to be sold from the name & Blood

Item I give a brindle Cowe to Brother, THOS:HARPR: & one thousand pounds of tobacco wch: THO: EVRT. & THO: BROWN standeth indebted to me by Bill

Item I give to MARY HARPR: ye Daught: of JNO: HARPR:, a brown Cow & calfe wth: their increase

Item I give a Cowe to JNO: HARPR: ye Son of Brother, JNO: HARPR:

Item I give my Horse to WM. LEAKE

Item I give to my beloved Brothr: JNO: HARPR:, whome I constitute mae & ordain my only & sole Exer. of this my last Will & Testament And I do hereby utterly disallow revoke & disannull all & very othr: formr: Testament Wills ratifying & confirming this & no othr: to be my last Will & Testament In Witness whereof I have hereunto set my hand & seale ye day & yeare above written

Signed sealed pronounced & declared by ye sd
SOLOMON HARPR: as his last Will & Testament
in pr:sence of us ye Subscribers SOLOMAN HARPR:
HANNAH RATLIFE her mark
JNO: KETH his mark
RICHD. COOPER

Proved in Essex County Court by ye oathes of HANNAH RATLIFE & JNO: KETH ye 10th day of 9ber: 1699 & truely recorded p FRANCIS MERIWETHER, Cl Cur

KNOW ALL MEN by these pr:sents that we JNO: HARPR: & RICHD. GREGORY both of the County of Essex are bound unto his Majties. Justices of ye peace of County of Essex in ye sum of Ten thousand pounds of tobacco & cask this 10th day of 9br: Anno Dom: 1699

The Condicon of this obligacon is that ye above bound JNO: HARPR: who at a Court held for Essex County ye day & yeare abovesd. obtained Probate of ye last Will of SOLOMAN HARPER; deced will perform & satisfie all such Legatees as are expressed & wt:soever ye Law enjoynes in such case, then ye above obligacon to be void otherwise to stand

Signed sealed & delivered in presents of us
THO: GREGSON, JON: HARPR:
ROBT. MOSELEY 1699 RICHD; GRIGORY

Truely recorded Test FRANCIS MERIWETHER, Cl Cur

p. IN YE NAME OF GOD Amen. I EDWARD THOMAS of Essex County in Virginia Gent.
21 doe make this my last Will and Testament in manner as followeth: Imprims: I bequeath my Soule to Almighty God who gave it me in sure and certaine hopes of Salvation through the meritts of my blessed Saviour Jesus Christ And my body to be burried in such decent Christian like manner as my friends hereafter named shall see fitt

Item It is my posetive will and desire that ye Estate belonging to ye Orphans of HEN: JONES & RICE JONES be first made good in kinde as I received itt out of my Estate

Item I give & bequeath unto Mrs. ELIZABETH MERRIWEATHER all that p:cell of land at ye Swamp where my Quarter is part of wch: I formerly bought of Mr. JNO: BRUSH wth: all houses Orchards and fenceing to her & her heirs for ever and all the stocke of cattle and hoggs that is upon ye sd Plantacon wth: four Negroes named James, Trigg, Scratch & Marrew wth: all their encrease to her ye sd Mrs. ELIZABETH ye Wife of Mr. THOMAS MERRIWEATHER to her and her heirs for ever

Item I lend unto my House Keeper, MARY PETERSON, ye use of five Negroes dureing ye terme of her life by name Semora & Doll, Jack and Booter and Moll and after her decease I bequeath ye saide five Negroes to my Executrs. hereafter named alsoe I lend her ye use of tht Plantacon called COXES QUARTER foure Cowes & calves & four Steeres three years old, two feather beddss & furneture, six pewter dishes and six plates, all this during her life

Item I give unto my Godson, THO: HILL, one Negroe boy called James

Item I give unto my Godson, CHARLES, ye Son of DANLL. DOBYNS, one Negroe girle caled Bess wth: all her Encrease

Item I give unto my Godson, caled WM. SMITH to buy him a Negroe twenty five pounds Sterling

Item I give unto EDWARD COLEMAN, ye Son of Mr. ROBT. COLEMAN, twenty five pounds to buy him a Negroe

Item I give & bequeath unto ye Pish of South Farnham for a GLEBE this Plantacon I now live on wth: all ye land houses orchards & fenceing thereunto belonging

Item I give & bequeath unto KATHERINE & FRANCES ye two younger Daughters of Mr. HENRY WILLIAMSON deceast all my other Estate either here or in England and doe appoint them to be my sole Executrixes of this my last Will & Testament Wittness my hand & seale this 23d of May 1699

Test DANLL. DOBYNS, EDWARD THOMAS
JON: JONES
ELIZABETH CHAMBRIDGE the marke of

Proved in Essex County Court ye 10th day of November 1699 by ye oathes of DANLL. DOBYNS & JON: JONES & ordered to be recorded Truely recorded FRANCIS MERIWETHER Cl

p. 22 September ye 2d 1699. Then appeared by us the Subscribers according to our Judgments in obedience to an Order from Essex County Court as followeth

2 cowes & calves, one Sword & pistoll, one young cow & heifer, one hand saw, branding iron, smoothing iron, one old horse saddle & bridle, one feathr: bed & bolster, one pr. of sheets & rugg, one p:cell of old iron, 2 chests, a parcell of pewter, one small box & case, a parcell of brass & tinware, one flock bed & covering, one Couch bed & one Chest, parcell of old wooden ware, 3 small potts & hookes, one hive of Bees, one frying pan, 2 pestles, one iron & one ladle, one Bill tobacco Five hundred and thirty, one small old gun, old pistole & one pair of fire tongs, 2 pr. of small stilliards, a percell of old bookes at 2 sh: 23:19:06

Sworne before me this 2d day of Septembr: 1699 GEORGE W TORNER
p RICHD. COVINGTON SAMLL. PARRY

Presented by JNO: BRACHER & ANN his Wife, Exec. of JONATHAN GRILL deced at a Court held for Essex County ye 10th day of 9br: 1699 upon Oath & truely recorded

p. 22 A true & perfect Inventory and account of as much of ye neat proceed of Seaven hhds. of tobo: Shipt. by Capt. ANTHONY SMITH deced in his life time on board ye *STEPHEN & EDWARD,* & consigned to Mr. JNO. COOPER, Merchant in LONDON, for sales as ever came to ye Custody or possession of me Subscriber & as may appear by sd COOPR:s Acct. Currant is as follows vizt.

1 Reame of fine writeing papr:, 2 fanns, 57 ells brown osneb; at 10 1/4 d. 21 ells wt. ditto at 11 d., 25 yds. 3/4 narr blew linnen at 7d., 20 yds narr ditto at 7d., 20 Ells wt. canvas at 10 1/2 d., 39 Ells broad canvas at 1s; one large looking glass, a Grazell, Mantua & petticoat, one ditto for one 15 years of age, one ditto, a pr. of Stayes, one ditto, 2 lutestring hoods at 61:4s; 2 wt. sarsnett ditto at 4:9:, 2 gawse hoods at 2:6; 65 foot Cutt glass, 40 foot turned lead, 2 lb. sawder, JOHN WEBSTER 16...11...10 1/4

Presented by JON: WEBSTER at a Court held for Essex County ye 10th day of 9ber: 1699 who made Oath that it is all ye Estate of ye sd deced not yet appraised that has come to his hands or knowledge and ye same is truely recorded. Test FRANCIS MERIWETHER Cl

p. 22 IN YE NAME OF GOD Amen. fourst beges my Soul to Almighty God wch: gave it me & my body to be boured wth: Christen bourel. I doe beques after ye deses of my Wife, ELEZEBETH GOUN my land to SARAH, Gran Daughter of SAMLL. GREEN to

her & Ars forever Wetness my hand the Sevon of July won thousen six noninty 8
CHARLES HALL JOHN I GOUNN
JOHN I PARR his marke
SAMLL. GREENE
Proved in Essex County Court ye 11th day of Novembr: 1699 by ye oathes of CHARLES HALL & SAML. GREENE witnesses hereto truely recorded. Test FRANCIS MERIWETHER Cl
Essex ss. The Deposition of SARAH ye Wife of SAMLL. GREENE aged forty yeares or there abouts sayth that yor: Deponant being at ye house of JNO. GUNN deceased ye night before his death for he died ye next night about the same time did here ye sd GUN desire my Husband to make his Will he being unwilling himselfe desired CHARLES HALL who then a FREEMAN in JNO: GUNs house to make itt tooke Inke & paper and yor: deponant did heare ye sd JNO: GUN dictate to ye Scribe verbatem that is written in ye Will & did see him Signe itt wth: his marke as itt appeares and yor: Depont. did take him ye sd GUN to be in perfict sence & memory at his signeing ye sd Will to ye best of my Judgment & knowledge & farther saith not
Examined & Sworne before me SARAH C GREENE
DANLL. DOBYNS
Truely recorded according to Ordr: of Essex County Court ye 11th day of 9br: 1699

pp. KNOW ALL MEN by these pr:sents that I THO: LANE of LONDON do hereby appoint
22- my loveing frind, THOM: COVINGTON, of Essex & Country of Virginia to be my
23 true & lawfull Attorney for me to demand recover & receive all such debts mony tobacco that is due to me by any means giveing my sd Attorney my whole power about ye premisses procuring of aney debts by action suit arrest & defend in any Courts of Law as ye cause may require touching me as my Agent or factor & wt:soever my sd Attorney shall do I do hereby confirme as if I ware parsonally present my selfe In Wittness whareof I have hearunto sett my hand & fixed my seale this 22th day of May Anno 1699
Signed sealed & delivered in ye presence of
RICH: COVINGTON, THO: LANE
JNO: KC CORP,
HENRY HP PURKINS
Proved by ye Oaths of JNO: CORPE & HENRY PIRKINS in Essex County Coart ye 13th day of 9br: 1699 & truely recorded Test FRANCIS MERIWETHER Cl Cur

p. Mr. THO: GREGSON. Sr. There is severall p:sons liveing in yor: parts indebted to
23 me I would desire you to receive ye same for me and in case of non paymt. to arest implead sett at liberty and discharge as you shall think fitt rattyfying & confirming what you shall doe or cause lawfully to be done about ye premisses to all intentes as though I was pr:sonally pr:sent and upon receipt to shipp ye same for BRISTOLL consigned to Mr. WM. FORNELL of Wine Street of BRESTOLL for my use this is all only that I am yor: freind & Servant
Westminstr: primo Aprill 1699 CHARLES HARFORD
To Mr. THO: GREGSON Practitioner in Law
in Essex County Virginia
These truely recorded Test FRANCIS MERIWETHER

p. Md. LEO: HILL haveing made complt. before me that ABRAHAM DEPREE standeth
23 justly indebted ye sume of Five pounds one shilliing Sterling money and Six hundred pounds of tobacco & being illegally gone out of the County, These are

therefore in his Majties. name to will and require you on sight hereof to attach soe much of ye Estate of ye sd ABRAHAM DEPREES as will satisfie the above sd: debt hereof faile not as you will answer ye Contrary. Given undr: my hand this 18th of 8br: 1699
To WILL: HUTTSON Constable or ye Sub Sheriff
to execute & make returne to ye next Court
held for this County DANLL. DOBYNS
The attachment executed ye first of November 1699 upon a parcell of tobacco and a parcell of Corne by me WILL: HUTTSON, Constable
Truely recorded Test FRANCIS MERIWETHER, Cl Cur

p. 23 These are to authorize and appoint yt: Mr. THO: COVINGTON for me & in my name to prosecute a certaine sute commenced and depending in Essex County Court agt: HENRY GOSLING to act and do for me and in my name as if I was there in my own proper person and for so doing this shal be yor: suffitient warrante as Witness my hand this tenth day of November Ano: Dom: 1699
Testes WM. JONES, MARY ST: H JOHNS
GEORGE LOYD Truely recorded

p. 23 Essex County ss. This day Capt. EDWARD MOSELEY made Complt. yt: JEREMIAH PARKER of this County stands indebted to him by Bill ye sume of One hundred & fifty pounds of tobo: & hath lately absented himselfe out of ye County
These are therefore in his Majties. name to will & requaire you to attach soe much of ye Estate of ye sd JEREM: PARKER as wilbe of value sufficient to satify ye sd Debt & ye same soe to secure yt: it may be lyable for satisfaction hereof faile not given undr: my hand this 11th: day of 8br: 1699
To ye High Sher: or his Deputy ROBT. BROOKE
to Exect & make returne
9ber: 11:th 1699. In Obedience to ye within Precept have attached as follows: two old iron potts wth: two holes in them & other old Lumber Pine
ROBT. MOSELEY Sub Sherif
Truely recorded FRANCIS MERIWETHER, Cl Cur

p. 23 Essex County. In Obedicne to an Ordr: of ye abovesd. County Court dated ye 11th: day of August 1699, wee ye Subscribers being sumond: and sworn by Mr. DANLL. DOBYNS did in obediance meete at ye House of WINSON WASSES', and did appraise such part of ye Estate of ROGER JONES deced as was attached by ye Sherif and offered before us in tobb: as followeth: Two small viceses, a parcell of old iron, a parcell of Smiths old togles, 3 pintells & brasses, 1 pr. of Smith bellow att a Small Chest & a small iron ptt:, 1 barron cow & 2 heifers - Eighteen pounds
Aprased the 3d day of Octobr: 1699 DANLL. WHITEHORNE
WM. YOUNG
JNO: WEBB
Truely recorded VINCENT VASS

pp. 23-24 Essex ss. Whereas Complaint hath been made this day before me by BRYANT TURNLEY that SAMLL. JACQUES late of this County, standeth indebted to him in ye summ of Eleaven hundred pounds of tobacco by Bill & Account & 4 barrells of Corn and hath absented himselfe out of ye County soe that no Course of Law can be had against him these are therefore in his Majties. name to will and require you to attach soe much of the Estate of ye sd JACQUES as shall satisffie ye debt and make report

thereof to ye next Court held for this County dated this 17th of August 1699
To ye High Sheriff of this County or his
Deputy to execute & returne JOHN CATLETT
Essex 7ber: ye 1st. 1699. Then Exeqt. this preceipt on ye Estate of SAM: JACQUES a crop of tobacco vallewd: at seaven hundred & fifetie pounds & seaven barlls: of Indyan Corne on Mr. BRYAN TURNLEYs Plantation wch: was appraised & sworne by Mr. CHARLES TALIAFERRO, Mr. AUGUSTIN SMITH & ROBT: SLAUGHTER of ye Viciridge given undr: my hand ye day & date p me ROBT. MOSELEY, Sub Sheriff of Essex County
CHARLES TALIAFERRO
AUGUSTINE SMITH
ROBT: R SLATER
Truely recorded Test FRANCIS MERIWETHER, Cl Cur

p. 24 7:br ye 11th: 1699 Sr: Please to speak to my business I have in Court against my Brothr: HAWKINS, ye Bill is inclosed. He will as I have heard bring 3 bushells of Salt against ye sd Bill at 100 p: bushell wch: I borrowed of him upwards of a twelve month agoe wch: cost him 25. p bushell ye Salt I am ready to pay him in kinde he doth this only to bread my hh. of toba: ye being wt: as pr:sent offers from yor: humble Servt. to Comd.
To Mr. THO: GRIGSON, WM. MOSELEY
These present truely recorded

p. 24 August 11th: 1699 Mr. GREGSON I request you to appear as my Attorney in action depending between me and ELIZABETH BRADLEY & for yor: soe doeing this shall be my sufficient warrent Witness my hand
To Mr. THO: GREGSON Attorney at Law AUGUSTIN SMITH
and for me alsoe CHARLES SMITH
Truely recorded Test FRANCIS MERIWETHER, Cl Cur

pp. 24-25 TO ALL CHRISTIAN PEOPLE to whome these pr:sents shall come wee JNO. HARPR: & LYDIA his Wife of ye County of Essex send greetings. Know yee that we ye sd JON: HARPR: & LYDIA his Wife for a valuable consideration to them in hand payd by SARAH NICHOLS of ye sd County, Widdow, and especially for ye sume of Two thousand One hundred pounds of tobacco and caske hath sold to SARAH NICHOLLS her heirs & assignes a certaiane p:cell of land being in ye aforesd. County being part of a greater divident formerly granted by Patent unto THOMAS HARPR: late of ye sd County deceased, wch: sd parcell of land is bounded as followeth: begininge at a willow Oake standing in ye Forke of a Swampe called by ye name of BRIDGE SWAMP issueinge out of PISCATAWAY CREEKE in ye sd County & Parrish of South Farnham, thence up ye sd Swamp to a white Oake standinge ye line of WM. COX & a longe ye sd line to a corner white Oake standinge by ye side of a small branch & thence down ye sd branch to a white Oake standinge in ye mouth of ye sd: branch & thence downe ye maine branch to ye sd Willo Oake where it began containeinge by estimacon One hundred acres of land together wthall houses plantations fences cleared grounds priviledges whatsoever to ye same belonging To have & to hold unto ye sd SARAH NICHOLLS her heires & assignes forever & ye sd JNO: HARPR: & LYDIA his Wife doth promise at all times for ever hereafter that she ye sd SARAH NICHOLLS her heires & assignes shall at all times forever hereafter peaceably hold ye sd land wthout any trouble of ye sd JNO: HARPR: or LYDIA his wife or any other p:sons claiminge thereunto payinge therefore unto ye Lord or Lords of ye Fees such rents & services as shall henceforth grow due In Wittness where-

of ye sd JNO: HARPR: & LYDIA his Wife have sett their hands & seales this Nineth day of Decembr: in ye yeare of our Lord One thousand Six hundred nynty & nine
Sealed & delivered in pr:sents of

ROBT. MOSELEY, JNO: HARPR:
THO: GREGSON LYDIA L HARPR:

Acknowledged & right of Dower relinquished idn Essex County Court ye 11th day of Xbr: 1699 & truely recorded Test FRANCIS MERIWETHER, Cl Cur

KNOW ALL MEN yt: I JNO: HARPR: of ye County of Essex, Planter, doe stand bound unto SARAH NICHOLLS of ye said County, Widdow, in ye just sum of Ten thousand pounds of tobac & caske good sound & merchantable sealed wth: my seale & dated ye nineth day of Decembr: Ano: Dom: 1699

The Condicon of this obligacon is that if JNO: HARPR: at all times truely keep all covenants that are or ought to be observed in a Deed of Sale between ye sd JNO: HARPR: & LYDIA his Wife & SARAH NICHOLLS accordinge to the meaninge of ye same That then this obligation to be void or else to stand in full force
Sealed & delivered in ye pr:sents of

ROBT. MOSELEY, JOHN HARPR:
THO: GREGSON

Acknowledged in Essex County Court ye 11th day of Xber: 1699 and truely recorded

p. 25 KNOW ALL MEN by these pr:sents that we JNO. SORRELL & JNO: WATERS of Essex County are firmly bound unto JNO: CATLETT, Gent., President of ye Court of ye sd County in ye sum of Ten thousand pounds of good tobac: & caske this 22d of Janry: 1699.

The Condicon of this obligacon is that if ye above bound JNO. SORRELL, Gardian of THO: INGRAM, Orphan of TOBIAS INGRAM deced, his heirs shall truely pay ye sd THO: INGRAM all such Estates shal come to ye hands of ye sd JNO: SORRELL as soon as ye sd THO. INGRAM shall attaine to lawfull age or when thereunto required by ye abovesd. County Court of Essex and keep harmless ye Justices of ye sd Court from all trouble & damages that may arise about ye sd Estate, Then ye above obligacon to be void otherwise to stand in full force
Signed sealed & delivered in pr:sence of us

FRA: MERAWATHER, JOHN SORRELL
JOHN MERRITT JOHN WATERS

Truely recorded Test FRANCIS MERIWETHER, Cl Cur

p. 25 Decembr: 4th: 1699. An Inventory of SOLLOMAN HARPR: Estate valued and oprayes by us ye Subscribours in obedience of an Order of Court dated ye 10th day of Novembr:

To one horse, one box, one flock bed & bolster rugg & blankett, 2000 eight paney nales, one Cow, one Cow & yearling, Six hundred pounds of tobo: in ye hand of WM. LACK, to fore hundred pound of tobo: in THO: hands 13...09...00 2000 tobacco

RICHD. R TILER
JNO: BURNETT
RICHD. GRIGORY

Presented at a Court held for Essex County ye 12th day of Xber: 1699 by JOHN HARPR:, Exr. of SOLLOMAN HARPR; deced upon Oath and truely recorded
Decembr: ye 4th day 1699 ye above appraisirs sworn by me JAMES BOUGHAN

p. 25 An Inventory of an apraisment of ye Estate of JEREMYAH PARKER praised pr. RICHD. GOODE SENR., JNO: MILLS, ROBT. MOSS.

Item to one Iron pott with a pease of brase on ye bottom of itt & a pare of pott hooks & some old Lumbr: to ye vallew of ninty pounds of tobacco this 8th day of December 1699 Truely recorded

pp. 25-26 KNOW ALL MEN by these pr:sents yt: wee ALICE SHIPLEY & WM. BENDRY of ye County of Essex are firmly bound unto JNO. CATLETT, Gent., President of ye Court in ye County sume of One hundred pounds Sterling money of England Witness our hands & seales this 10th day of Aprill Anno Dom: 1700

The Condition of this obligation is that if ye ALICE SHIPLEY, Admrstrx. of all goods chattells & credits of DANL. SHIPLEY deced do make perfect Inventory of all ye goods cattles & credits of the sd deceasded as shall come to ye hands of her ye said ALICE SHIPLEY and to exhibit to ye next Court & make Oath thereto & truely administer according to Law & cause to be made a true & just accot. of her Admcon. when thereunto lawfully required & pay unto such persons as ye sd Court shall appoint then this obligation to be void else to remain in full force

Signed sealed & delviered in pr:sence of

ROBT. MOSELEY, ALICE (mark) SIPPLEY

FRA: MERIWETHER WM. BENDERY

Truely recorded Test FRANCIS MERIWETHER, Cl Cur

p. 26 THIS INDENTURE made ye 24th day of August 1699 between THO: FLOYD of Feirsh: aged about Thirteen years on ye one part & RICHD. BRIDGE of LEVERPOOLE, Mercht. on ye other part; Witnesseth that ye sd THO: FLOYD doth hereby agree wth: ye sd RICHD: BRIDGE his heirs & assignes from ye day of ye date hereof until his first & next arrivall at Virginia or MARYLAND & after for & during ye tearme of Eight yeares to serve in such service & employments as he ye sd RICHD. BRIDGE or his assignes shall there employ him in according to ye custome of ye Country in ye like kind, In Consideration whereof sd RICHD. BRIDGE doth hereby grant to pay for his passage and to find & allow him meat drink apparrell & lodging wth: other necessaries according to ye Custome of ye Country in ye like kind, In Wittness whereof ye p:ties to these pr:sents have hereunto interchangeably sett their hands and seales ye day and yeare above written

Sealed & delivered in pr:sence of

JA: BENN, Dept. Mayr: Leverpoole THO: (mark) FLOYD

JNO: SANDFORD, Not: Pub.

We arrived in Virginia ye twenty second of 9ber: in ye *LAMB of LEVERPOOLE* as Wittness my hand WM. EVERED, Mastr: of the aaforesaid *LAMB*

Rappahannock March ye ddddd9th: 1699. I doe assigne the within mentioned Servant to Mrs. ALICE SHIPLEY or her assignes as wittness my hand WM. EVERED

Truely recorded according to an Ordr: of Essex County Court ye 10th day of Aprill 1699

p. 26 IN THE NAME OF GOD Amen. I WM: MOSELEY of ye County of Essex being sicke weake in body but of sound & perfect memory praised be God for ye same Calling to mind ye uncertainty of this transitory life that all flesh must yeild unto death when itt shall please God to call, doe make constitute and ordaine this my last Will & Testament in manner & forme following.

First I give & bequeath my Soul to Got yt: gave itt in hopes of a joyfull resurrection at ye last Day & my body to ye Earth to be decently interred after my decease, & as to my temporall Estate wherewth: itt hath pleased God to bless me I will & bequeath ye same in mannr: & forme following

First, I will & bequeath ye plantation and land whereon I now live withall ye houses orchards buildings & all other appurtenances thereunto belonging to my Son, WILLIAM MOSELEY & his heirs forever

Item I will & bequeath my quarter plantation being Two hundred acres as by Deed may appeare being purchased ut of a divident of land commonly called BUTTONS RAINGE unto my Son, JNO: MOSELEY, wth: all ye buildings houses & appurtenances thereto belonging to him & his heirs forever

Item I will & bequeath all my lands lyeing nigh or upon GILSONS RUN taken up by Pattent between my Honord. Father & NICHO: CATLETT to my two Sons, WM. MOSELEY & JNO: MOSELEY equally to be divided between them to them & their heirs forever

Item I will & bequeath all my p:sonal Estate goods cattells & Chattles unto my two Sons, WILL: & JNO:MOSELEY & my Daughtr: MARTHA MOSELEY, to be equally divided betweene them except one Silver Tankard, one Silver Porringer & Ten Silver Spoones wch: I give unto my Daughtr: MARTHA, p:ticularly above her equal share wth: her Brothrs: & if any of my said Children, Wm:, JNO: & MARTHA MOSELEY happen to dye before they attaine to age or marry then my will is yt: his or her part shall returne to ye Survivors equally.

Lastly, I nominate & appoint my Son, WM. MOSELEY, Executr: of this my last Will & Testament & do nominate my three Brothrs: EDWARD, ROBT., & BENJAMIN MOSELEY Overseers & doe desire them to see this my Will performed & imediately after my decease to returne an Inventory of all my p:sonall Estate into ye Court & my will is that my Estate may not be kept intire as now itt is & that my Children receive their parts & portions respectively as they attaine to ye age of Eighteen yeares or marry wch: shal first happen & I doe desire my three Brothrs: aforesd. to see & take care yt: all my Children be brought up to good learning out of their Estate

Item I will unto my Brothr:, EDWD. MOSELEY, my Coate vest & breeches wch: I daily weare wth: ye great Coate belonging to them

Item I will unto my Brothr:, ROBT. MOSELEY, my new broad cloth Coate wth: Druggett vest & breeches

Item I give unto my Son, WILLIAM, my Sadle holstr: & pistolls & great Sword wth: my horse, Dick, & to my Son, JNO:, I give my little Sword &m Gaggonett wth: a horse when he is capable to ride & I give to my two Sons my two gold rings wch: I usually weare & to my Daughtr: MARTHA, ye three weding gold rings wch: was her Mothers

Item I give unto my Neighbor, REBECCA STOKES, one suite of my wifes apparrell from head to foot none excepted but ye Crape gowne & petty coate & likewise six hundred pounds of tobo:; it being for her extraordinary care & payns in mine & my Wifes sickness

Item I give unto my Godson, WM. JONES, one Ewe to be delivered att ye Inventory of ye Estate & her increase to be towards his Schooling

Item I give one Ewe more upon ye same Act. unto WILL: Son of ROBT. BROOKE

Item I give unto my Servant, ED: COSE, one heifer of two years old & I doe declare this to be my last Will & Testamt. & no other. In Testimony whereof I have hereto put my hand & seale this 6th day of January 1699

Signed sealed & delivered in ye pr:sence of

GEORGE TAYLER, WM. MOSELEY
ROBT. BROOKE,
ROBT. MOSELEY 1699

Proved by ye Oathes of ye Wittnesses hereto in Essex County Court ye 16th day of Aprill 1700 & truely recorded Test FRANCIS MERIWETHER, Cl Cur

p. THIS INDENTURE made ye 7th day of Septembr: 1699 betweene JACOB SHERWOOD
27 of Attorehow in Cheshire aged about thirteen yeares on ye one part & RICHD.
BRIDGE of LEVERPOOLE, Mercht., on ye other part Wittnesseth tht ye sd JACOB SHERWOOD doth hereby agree wth: ye sd RICHD. BRIDGE his heires & assignes from ye day of ye date hereof until his first & next arrivall at Virginia or MARYLAND & aftr: for & during the tearme of Eight yeares to serve in such service & employmt. as he ye sd RICHD. BRIDGE shall employ him in according to ye custome of ye Countrey in ye like kind, In Consideracon ye sd RICHD. BRIDGE doth grant t pay for his passage & to find & allow him meat drink aparrell & lodging wth: all necessarys according to ye Custome of ye Countrey. In Wittness whereof ye p:ties to these pr:sents have sett their hands & seales ye day & yeare above written

Sealed & delivered in ye pr:sence of
THO: SWEETING, Mayr. de LEVERPOOLE, JACOB SHERWOOD
JNO: SANDFORD Not: Publ:

We arived in Virginia ye twenty second of 9ber: 1699

KNOW ALL MEN by these pr:sents that WM. ALLEN doe assigne all my right title interest and claime of in & unto a man Servant named JACOB SHERWOOD unto THO: HUSCLESCOTT his heirs Executrs. and Admrs. as Wittness my hand this 2d: day of January 1699 old Stile

Teste WM. X PLUMR: WM. ALLEN
RICHD. GRAVES

Truely recorded according to Ordr: of Essex County Court ye 10th day of April 1700

p. THIS INDENTURE made ye Ninth day of 9ber: 1699 Between JNO: EDWARDS of
27 DERBYSHIRE aged about Eighteen yeares on ye one part & LEWIS JENKINS of
LEVERPOOLE, Mercht. on ye other parte. Wittnesseth that the sd JNO: EDWARDS doth agree wth: ye sd LEWIS JENKINS his heirs or assigns from ye day of ye date hereof until his first & next arrivall in Virginia or MARYLAND, and after during ye terme of Six yeares to serve in such service & employmt. as he ye sd. LEWIS JENKINS or his assignes shall here employ him in according to ye Custome of ye Countrey in ye like kind. In Consideration whereof ye sd LEWIS JENKINS doth grant wth: ye sd JNO: EDWARDS to pay for his passage & to find & allow him meate drink apparrell & lodging wth: other necessaries acording to ye Custome of ye Countrey In Wittness whereof ye parties to these pr:sents have hereunto sett their hands & seales ye day & year above writtin

Sealed & delivered in pr:sence of
CUTH: ST. HARPLES, Mayr. de LEVERPOOLE, LEWIS JENKINS
JNO: LANSFORD, Not: Pub

This Servants time begun ye 19th day of Feb: 1699/1700

And I do assigne ye sd Servant wthin menshoned JNO: EDWARDS unto Mr. PETER BROOKES, Planter, in Virginia as Wittness my hand this 8th day of March 1699/1700

Truely recorded according to Ordr: of Essex County Court ye 10th day of Aprill 1700

pp. THIS INDENTURE made ye tenth day of October in ye yeare of our Lord God One
27- thousand six hundred Ninety and nine Betweene JOHN HAWKINS of the Parish of
29 Cittenbourne in ye County of Essex, Planter, onely Sonne & heir of THOMAS
HAWKINS late of ye same Parish and County, Gent., deced, of ye one part and BARTHOLOMEW VAWTER of ye Parish and County aforesaid, Planter, of ye other part Witnesseth that for ye sume of Nine thousand pounds of good sound marchantable tobacco unto the said JOHN HAWKINS in hand paid he doth hereby sell unto the said

BARTHOLOMEW VAWTER his heires and assignes forever all that parcell of land containeing One hundred and Fifty cres being in the Parish of Cittenburne and County of Essex aforesd., being part of a Dividend of land granted to Mr. THOMAS LUCAS by Pattent bearing date the 16th of December 1663, And afterwards by an Escheat granted to ye above said THOMAS HAWKINS by Pattent bearing date the Sixth day of Octobr: 1675, the said land lyeing at the head of a Creeke formerly called Mr. LUCASES CREEK, begining at a red Oake corner tree standing at the Westermoste end of ye back line of the aforesd. Pattent & runeth thence North West to the aforesd. Creeke by and nigh the OLD ROAD at the place of going over comonly called the LONG BRIDGE, And thence down the sd Creeke North East and thence North East to ye mouth of a branch that falleth into ye sd Creeke, thence up ye sd branch South West to a marked white Oake standing in a forke of the sd branch nigh the LOWER ROAD that leadeth downe the River and thence crossing the sd ROAD South West to ye aforesd. back line, and thence North West to ye first menconed red Oake, the said One hundred & Fifty acres of land now doth of right belong unto the said JOHN HAWKINS as Sonne and heir of the said THOMAS HAWKINS deced as aforesd., with all houses buildings barnes rivers timber appurtenances belonging and all the right & demand of the said JOHN HAWKINS to the same; To have & to hold the sd Land with all rights kunto the sd BARTHOLOMEW VAWTER his heirs and assignes forever performing the services wch: shall hereafter grow due in respect of the pr:misses unto our Soveraigne Lord the King the said JOHN HAWKINS his heirs & assigns will warrant & for ever defend against molestation of any person whatsoever In Wittness whereof ye parties first above named their hands & seales have interchangeably sett
Signed sealed & delivered in pr:sence of

JOHN PEATLE, JOHN HAWKINS
EDWARD GOULDMAN

Acknowledged by JNO: HAWKINS abovesd. & right of Dower relinquished by ELIZ: his Wife in Essex County Court ye 10th day of Aprill 1700 & truely recorded

KNOW ALL MEN that I JNO. HAWKINS, Planter, am bound unto BARTHOLOMEW VAWTER in ye sum of One hundred & fifty pounds lawfull money of England ye tenth day of Octobr: in year One thousand six hundred ninety and nine

The Condicon of this obligation is if the sd. JNO: HAWKINS truely keep all covenants in one Indenture between JNO: HAWKINS of one part & BARTHOLOMEW VAWTER of ye other part according to ye intent of sd Indenture Then this obligacon to be void or else to remain in full force

Sealed & delivered in pr:sence of

JNO: BOULWARE, JNO: HAWKINS
SIMD SB BOULLIN

Acknowledged ye 10th day of Aprill 1700 in Essex County Court & truely recorded

p. 29 THIS INDENTURE made this (blank) day of (blank) in ye yeare of our Lord God One thousand seven hundred & in the twelft yeare of ye Reigne of our Sovereign Lord William the Third &c., over England Scotland France Ireland & Virginia, King &c., Betweene CHARLES COMBES of ye County of Essex, Planter, of ye one part & JNO: ALEXANDER of ye same County, Turner, of ye other pte:, Witnesseth that ye sd CHARLES COMBES for a valuable consideration in hand already reced have sold unto ye sd JNO: ALEXANDER his heirs & assignes all his right unto certain p:cell of land being in ye County of Essex aforesd. & given unto ye sd CHARLES COMBES by WM. VEALE late of ye sd County of Essex deced in his last Will & Testiment, bearing date ye 29th: of May Anno 1693 & proved before ye Worpfull: Justices holding Court for ye sd Countie of Essex February ye 10th 1693; To have & to hold ye sd land wth: all woods waters thereunto belonging subject to the quitte rents that shall grow due and ye sd CHARLES COMBES for ye sd valuable consideracon ye sd land hereby granted will defend sd JNO. ALEXANDER his heirs & assignes forever from him his heirs or any other persons laying any claim & ye sd CHARLES COMBES doth further grant to execute & due acknowledgement of ye premisses before ye Justices hold Court for ye above mentioned County of Essex and there to be enrolled according to ye Statute in yt: case made & provided, In Wittness of all & singular ye Articles concerning ye premisses ye sd CHARLES COMBES hath sett his hand & fixed his seale

Signed sealed & delivered in pr:sents of us
JOHN PEADLE CHARLES X COMBES
THO: HUCKLESCOTT

Acknowledged in Essex County Court ye 10th day of Aprill 1700 & truely recorded

pp. 29-30 KNOW ALL MEN that I FRANCIS GIBSON (Sonne & heir of WM. GIBSON deced) of ye Parish of Sittingborne in ye County of Essex do by these pr:sents for three thousand five hundred pounds of tobo: by HENRY LONG of ye same Pish: have granted & sold a tract of land being on ye South side of Rappa: River containing One hundred forty two acres & a halfe being one moyety of a Pattent granted RICHD. WEST & ROGER CLOTWORTHY for Two hundred Eighty five & a halfe acres of land & by ye sd RICHD. WEST sold to ye sd WM. GIBSON, ye sd part be lyeinge on ye upper side of a line of marked trees wch: divides ye whole Pattent; unto ye sd HENRY LONG his heires & assignes for ever with all its rights houses gardens orchards wood & appurtenances belonging; To have & to hold to him forever & I ye sd FRANCIS GIBSON for my selfe my heires will warrant forever from ye claimes of any persons whatsoever to peaceably occupy ye sd land at all times forever lawfully & peaceably wthout trouble of me my heires or other p:sons lawfully claimeing In Wittness I have sett my hand & seale this eleventh day of March 1699/1700

Signed sealed & delivered in ye pr:sence of
ROBT. HALSEY, FRANCIS F GIBSON his marke
WM. AYRES

Acknowledged in Essex County Court ye 10th day of Aprill 1700 & truely recorded

p. 30 TO ALL &c. wherein &c. Now know yee that I ye sd Sr. EDMOND ANDROS Knt. their Majties. Lieut. & Governor Generall &c. doe wth: ye advice & consent of ye Councill of State accordingly give & grant unto JNO. MAGUFFEY Seaventy seaven acres of land scituate in Essex County bounded as followeth begining at a corner hiccory in a branch of GILSONS CREEKE corner of Mr. EDMOND (   ) line & runing West by North by sd PAGGITTs land Four hundred & forty poles to a stake in an Old Feild, thence North by East to sd TANDEYs land to a corner white Oake on GILSONs Maine Pocoson, thence by his line South East to the begining place, ye said land being due unto ye sd JNO. MAGUFFEY for ye importation of two p:sons into this Colony whose names are to be in ye Records mentioned under this Patent To have & to hold &c. To be held &c. Yeilding and paying &c. Provided &c. Given under my hand & ye Seale of ye Colony this Twenty nineth day of Aprill in ye Fifth year of ye Reign of our Sovereigne Lord & Lady, William and Mary of England &c. Annoq Dom: 1693

A Patent for 77 acres of land in Essex
granted to JOHN MAGUFFY RALPH WORMELEY Secr. E. ANDROS

KNOW ALL MEN by these pr:sents that I ye within mentioned JNO. MAGUFFY for ye consideration of Seven hundred pounds of good sound tobacco in hand already re- ceived whereof I doe hereby acknowledge assigne over all my right & claim of ye wthin mentioned Patent unto JOSEPH CALLAWAY his heires & assigns forever wth: warranty from all & every p:sons wt:soever As Wittness my hand this 10th day of Aprill 1700

Test WM: T DIAR, JOHN ⊠ MAGUFFE
THO: HUCKLESCOTT

Acknowledged in Essex County Court ye 10th day of Aprill 1700 and truely recorded

p. 30 KNOW ALL MEN by these presents that wee JOHN BROOKE, THO: COVINGTON & HENRY GOARE are firmly bound unto JNO: CATLETT Gent., President of ye County Court in ye sum of One hundred pds. Ster. money of England this 10th day of Aprill 1700

The Condition of ye obligationis if ye above bounden JNO: BROOKE, Administrator of all & singular goods & credits of RICHD: (faded) cause to be made a true Inventory of all goods chattells & credits of ye sd deced wch: come to hands of him ye sd JNO. BROOKE & exhibit to ye next Court & make Oath thereto & further do make a true and full accot. of his admicon. when lawfully required and all ye rest of ye sd goods & credits which shall be found remaineing being first examined and allowed shall deliver & pay unto such persons as ye sd Court shall appoint, Then this obligation to be void & non effect or else to remaine in force

Signed sealed & delivered in ye pr:sence of
THO: GREGSON, JNO: BROOKE
FRA: MERIWETHER THOMAS COVINGTON
Truely recorded HENRY GOARE

p. 30 Ann Acount of what I received of BENJAMEN MASH deets to 1 mare & colt, to 440 pounds of tobo: reced: att times TIMOTHY DRISCOLL
Truely recorded Test FRANCIS MERIWETHER, Cl Cur

p. 30 SS Virginia August ye 6th 1698 125 lb:
Forty dayes after sight of this my third Bill of Excha: my first & second not paid pay unto Mr. JNO. HAWKINS or order One hundred twenty five pounds Sterling for value here received of him at the time make good paymt. & place it to accot. of yor: Servt.

To Mr. MICAJAH PERRY & COMPA: DOROTHY H HORTH her mark
Merchts. in LONDON

Truely recorded according to an Order of Essex County Court ye 10th day of Aprill 1700

pp. 30-31 THIS INDENTURE made ye 24th day of August 1699 Between WM. EDMONDS of DERBYSHIRE aged about twelve yeares on ye one part & RICHD. BRIDGE of LEVERPOOLE Mercht., Wittnesseth that ye sd WM. EDMONDS doth hereby agree from day of ye date hereof untill his first & next arrivall at Virginia or MARYLAND & during ye tearme of Twelve yeares to serve in such service as he ye sd RICHD. BRIDGE or his assignes shall there employ him according to ye Custome of ye Country In Consideration whereof ye sd RICHD. BRIDGE doth hereby agree to pay for his passage & to find & allow him meat drink apparrel & lodging wth: other necessarys according to ye custome of ye Country. In Wittness ye p:ties hve sett their hands & seales

Signed sealed & delivered in ye pr:sence of
JA: BENN Dept. Mayr: de LEVERPOOLE WM. E EDMONDS
JNO. LANDFORD

We arrived in Virginia ye Twenty second of 9ber: 1699
WM. EVERED, Commandr: of ye *LAMB* Liverpoole

Truely recorded according to an Ordr: of Essex County Court the 10th of Aprill 1700
Rappahannock March ye 11th 1699. I doe assigne ye within mentioned Servant to ANN MORTON, Widdow, or her assignes as Wittness my hand ye day & year above writen

WM. EVERED

Truely recorded Test FRANCIS MERIWETHER, Cl Cur

p. 31 IN THE NAME OF GOD, Amen. I ANTHONY NORTH being sick & weake in body but of sound & perfect Memory blessed & praised be Almighty God for ye same, do make & ordain this to be my last Will & Testament in manner & form following;

First & principally I comend my Soul into the hands of Almighty God who gave it hopeing by ye Merites & death & passion of or: blessed Lord & Saviour Jesus Christ to receive full pardon & forgiveness of all my Sinns & offences & a joyfull resurrection at ye last Day; As for ye worldly goods that God of his Mercy hath lent I will I bequeath them in manner following;

Imprimis I give & bequeath to my Grandson, ANTHONY NORTH, Two hundred acres of high land being Woodland & Fiftie acres of Marish land & when my sd Grandson shall come to age, I give him my Bell metle pestle & mortar

Item I give & bequeath to my Grand Daughter, JEAN NORTH, Seventy acres of high land where my Son, ABRAM NORTH lived, & thirty acres of Marish land & my Silver Sack Cupp & two cowes & their encrease ye one named Brindle ye other Cherry

All ye rest of my Estate reall & personall after my debts & funerall charges pd. & discharged, I give and bequeath to my son, WILLIAM NORTH, and his heires

And I do make my Son, WM. NORTH, full & whole Executor of this my last Will and Testament utterly revokeing annulling & makeing void all former Wills, testaments, legacies or bequests by me at any time heretofore made given or bequeathed and publish declare & pronounce this as my last Will and Testament. In Wittness whereof I have hereunto sett my hand & seale this 24th day of February 1699/1700

Signed seald published declared & pronounced to be ye last Will & Testament of ye sd ANTHONY NORTH in pr:sence of us JNO: WAGGONER,
JOHN I HOW,
THO: HUCKLESCOTT

ANTHONY AN NORTH

Prov'd by ye Oathes of JNO: WAGGONER & THO: HUCKLESCOTT in Essex County Court ye 10th day of Aprill 1700 & truely recorded Test FRANCIS MERIWETHER, Cl Cur

p. 31 Feby. ye 10th 1699. The Deposicon of JUDITH DAVIS aged 27 years or thereabouts being examd. & sworne saith yt: upon ye 9th of this Instant of goeing to ye house of THO: DAYES of Farnham Parish in Essex County at ye request of MARY HODGES her Neighbour & seeing ye sd DAYES Wife lying dead upon ye bed in a most horied & barboris manner all gored & blood this Dept. asked how his Wife came to be in that condicon who made answer he knew not; This Depont. further asked him if he & his Wife had been quarrelling who replyed yt: he & his Wife had not had an angry word this many a day, also this Depont. further asked him if anybody had been lately there who answered noe nither did he see any body; also this Depont. asked him how he burnt his eyes, who replyed against ye pott rack & being asked a little while after by this Depont. how he hurt himselfe, he answered ye Lord knowes I know not & this Depont. saith further that ye sd THO: DAY had then at ye same time his face & eyes most greveously brused & further saith not

Sworne before me ye day & yeare above written
RICHD. COVINGTON

JUDITH X DAVIS

In ye place of Coroner Truely recorded Test FRANCIS MERIWETHER, Cl Cur

Essex County ss. AN INQUISITION indented and taken at ye House of THOMAS DAYES in Farnham Parish in Essex County ye 10th day of February in ye yeare 1699 before me, RICHD. COVINGTON, one of his Majties. Justice of ye Peace for ye County of Essex. upon view of ye body of ELIZABETH DAY, ye Wife of THOMAS DAY, then & there lying dead & ye sd Juries being good and lawfull men and sworne to trye & inquire in ye behalfe of our Sovereigne Lord ye King how & in what manner ye sd ELIZA: DAY came by her death & they upon their Oathes say that ye sd ELIZABETH DAY was much beaton & brused with both her eyes extreme black wth: many other bruses on her face & a bruse on her right Eare & a hold undr: neath ye same Eare & we of the Jurors say was ye cause of ye sd ELIZA: DAYs death & wee of ye Jurors further day that THO: DAY at ye same time was much brused and beaten haveing both his eyes extremely brused & black & several cuts in his head & further upon his examination would not confess anything how ELIZABETH his Wife came by them blowes & wounds nor how he came to be so beaten himselfe so we ye Jurors say that in ye Parrish & County aforesd. on ye Eighth or Ninth of this Instant Febr: in ye Dwelling House of sd THO: DAY, that ye sd ELIZA: was barbarosly murdered & by all manner of circumstances we can find or geather that ye aforesd. THOM: DAY is guilty of ye murdering ye said ELIZABETH DAY

In Refferance to ye same, I RICHD. COVINGTON, as aforesd. togeather with ye Jurors aforesd., have put our hands & seales ye day & date above written

RICHARD COVINGTON
in ye place of Coroner

SAMLL. PARRY	THO: EWETT	HENRY I X PERKINS
RICHD. R TAYLER	THO: O CRANCK	THO: ⊢ JOHNSONE
THO: GREENE	WM: M PRICE	SAMLL. COATES
JOHN BROOKS	THO: S COOPER	HENRY GOARE
JEFFREY I DYER	THO: T WILLIAMSON	

Truely recorded FRANCIS MERIWETHER, Cl Cur

February ye 10th 1699. The Deposition of ELIZABETH ACRES aged thirty eight years or thereabout being examined & sworne saith yt: upon ye Ninth of this Instant that going to ye House of THO: DAYs of Farnham Parrish in Essex County at ye request of MARY HODGE, her Neighbour, & seeing ye sd DAYs Wife lying dead upon ye bed in a most horred & barbours manner all gored in blood, this Deponent asked how his Wife came to lie in that condition who made answer he knew not; this Depont. further asked him if he & his Wife had been quarrelling, who replyed yt: he & his Wife had not had an angry word this many day; Also this Depont. further asked him if any body had been lately there, who answered no neither did he see anybody; also this Depont. askt. him how he hurt his eyes who replyed against ye potrac & being asked a litle while after by this Depont. how he hurt himselfe, he answered ye Lord knows I know not, & this Depont. saith further yt: the sd THOMAS DAYE had then at ye same time his face & eyes most greviously brused wth: severall wounds & bruses upon his head and further saith not Sworne before me ye day & yeare above written

by me RICHD. COVINGTON in ye place of a Coroner ELIZABETH X ACRES

Truely recorded Test FRANCIS MERIWETHER, Cl Cur

The Deposition of MARY HODGES, aged Seaventy six yeares or thereabouts being examined & sworne saith yt: upon ye ninth of this Instant coming from ye house of Mr. THO: COVINGTONs & going to THO: DAYs of Farnham Pish, in Essex County seeing ye sd DAY setting upon ye Couch by ye fire some wt. melancholy asked him how he did, who answered he did not know his face & eyes being most greviously brused, he presently after tould me yt: his Wife was dead. Your Depont. asked him how she came to die, who presently replyed she about two houres before day yt: morning. Your Depont. further asked him how his face came to be in yt: condition, who tould me he cut it against ye pottracks yt: was over ye fire; upon wch: I went to ye Woman, his Wife, as she lay on ye bed & found her dead. Your Depont. seeing her lye in a most horred & barborous maner all gored in blood upon wch: your Depont. took her feet and found her legg to be some what limber. Ye sd DAY requesting her to strip her dead body, I tould him I was not able of myselfe to perform it. She further tould him I would goe for more assistance & call of JUDITH DAVIS, his Daughter in Law, & ELIZABETH ACRES, wch: accordingly I did & yor: Depont. further saith not

Sworne before me ye day & year above written

RICHD. COVINGTON in place of Coroner MARY X HODGES

Truely recorded Test FRANCIS MERIWETHER, Cl Cur

p. 32 THE AGREEMENT made this 19th of 7br: 1699 Between JNO: BREDGAR, Mariner, of ye one parte & FRA: THORNTON & JNO: BATTAILE of ye other part; Wittnesseth that sd JNO: BREDGAR hath sold to ye sd THORNTON & BATTAILE their heires & assignes two parcells of land being in ye freshes of Rappa: River & bequeathed by WM. CREYTON & THO: CREYTON to ye sd BREDGAR & to ELIZA: his Wife, wch: said land ye sd BREDGAR doth oblidge himselfe his heires or his Attorney well impowered he will a good title & estate in fee simple make in ye County Court. In Consideracon of ye above premisses ye sd BATTAILE & THORNTON do hereby oblige themselves of &c. yt: upon acknowledgemt: if ye above sd Deed for ye land to give & delivr: to ye BREDGAR or Ordr: good & sufficient Bills of Exchange for One hundred pounds Sterling money of England In Wittness whereof ye sd parties to these pr:sents have sett their hands & seales

Test WM. ROBINSON, JNO: BREDGAR

FRA: STONN FRA: THORNTON

I doe acknowledge to have reced of ye abovesd BATTAILE & THORNTON in parte of ye abovesd. sume & in confirmacon hereof, one pound in hand at ye sealing and signing of ye above Agreemt. Wittness my hand 7ber: ye 19th 1699. JOHN BRIDGAR

Truely recorded according to Order of Essex County Court ye 10th day of Aprill 1700

TO ALL XTIAN PEOPLE to whom this pr:sent writing shall come, I FRANCIS STONE of ye County of RICHMOND in Virginia by vertue of an Instrument of Writeing under ye hand & seales of JNO: BREDGAR & ELIZABETH BREDGAR his Wife bearing date ye tenth of Novembr: Anno Dom: 1697, proved & recorded in RICHMOND County authorized & impowered to sell & dispose of all land houses estates rights & titles or plantacons wt:soever wherein they are concerned as Legatees & Exexr. of ye last Will & Testament of THO: CRIGHTON deced bearing date ye 5th: of Novembr: 1694, lyeing and being in Virginia; & doe for & on ye behalfe & in ye name of ye sd JNO. BREDGAR & ELIZA: his Wife, or as their Attorney, send greeting in or: Lord God everlasting this Eleventh day of March in ye yeare of our Lord One thousand six hundred Ninty nine. Now know yee that I ye sd FRA: STONE for and on ye behalfe & in ye names of ye sd JNO: & ELIZA: BREDGAR for & in consideration of Fifty pounds Sterling money in hand paid to me for ye use of ye sd. JNO: & ELIZA: BREDGAR by JNO: BATTAILE of Essex County in Virginia have granted one tract of land containing Seven hundred acres more or less being on ye South side of Rappa: in ye freshes thereof, being part of a greater tract of land granted to HENRY CRIGHTON & JNO: PROSSER, one moyety belonging to ye sd HENRY CRIGHTON & given to his three Sons, HENRY, WILLIAM & THOMAS CRIGHTON, by Will baring date ye 26th of Janry: 1676; unto ye sd JNO. BATTAILE his heires & assignes for ever with all its rights gardens orchards to ye same belonging being ye lower most parte of ye sd HENRY CRIGHTONs moyety & ye full parte belonging to ye sd THO: CRIGHTON by his sd. Father Last Will & Testament; To have & to hold ye sd tract of land with appurtenances unto him ye sd JNO. BATTAILE his heires & assignes forever to quietly hold said tract of land wthout any trouble whatsoever. In Wittness whereof ye sd FRA: STONE for ye sd JNO. BREDGAR & ELIZA: his Wife & as their Attorney have sett my hand & fixed my seale

Signed sealed & delivered in ye pr:sence of us

WILLIAM COLSTON, FRA: STONE
SAMLL. SALLIS
ROBT. COLEMAN

Acknowledged in Essex County Court ye 10th day of Aprill 1700 & truely recorded

pp. 33 TO ALL XTIAN PEOPLE to whome these pr:sents shall come, I FRA: STONE of Sittingburne Parish in ye County of RICHMOND in Virginia: beinge constituted & impowered by JNO: BREDGAR & ELIZA: his Wife both of ROTHIRITH in ye County of SURREY in ye Kingdom of England by an Instrument of Writeing bearing date ye tenth of November 1697 proved in RICHMOND County Court ye 1st of Novembr: 1699 & recorded to sell & dispose of all land, houses, estates, rights & titles in Virginia to ye sd JNO: and ELIZABETH belonging accrueing by ye last Will & Testament of WM. CRIGHTON deced late of ye Pish of ROTHIRITH in ye County of SURREY bearing date the 5th of February Anno Dom 1695 for & on ye behalfe & in ye name of ye sd JNO: & ELIZA: BREDGAR his Wife for & in consideration of Fifty pounds Sterling money in hand paid to me FRANCIS STONE for ye use of ye sd JNO: & ELIZA: BREDGAR by FRA: THORNTON of RICHMOND County in Virginia and by these presents in ye names of ye abovesd. JNO: & ELIZA: BREDGAR doe fully sell tract of land containing Seven hundred acres more or less to ye sd FRA: THORNTON his heires & assignes forever ye sd land on ye South side of Rappa: River in ye freshes thereof, being parte of a certain tract of land granted by Pattent to HENRY CRIGHTON & JNO: PROSSER one moyety belonging to ye sd HENRY CRIGHTON & given to his three Sonns HENRY, WILLIAM & THOMAS CRIGHTON, by Will bearing date ye 26th of Janry; 1676 with all and singular its rights all gardens orchards pastures to ye same belonging this being ye upper part of they three; To have and to hold ye sd tract of land unto him ye sd FRAN: THORNTON his heires & assignes forever clearly acquitted from all manner of gifts sales & singular othr: troubles demands & Incumbrances wt:soever to ye sd FRANCIS THORNTON at all times forever hereafter lawfully & quietly to hold without any trouble of ye sd JNO: BREDGAR, ELIZA: BREDGAR their or eithr: of their heires In Witness whereof ye sd FRAN: STONE for & on behalfe of ye sd JNO: BREDGAR, ELIZA: BREDGAR & as their Constituant & Attorney have sett my hand & seale this Eleventh day of March 1699/1700

Signed sealed & delivered in ye pr:sence of us

WM. COLSTON, FRA: STONE
SAMLL. SALLES
ROBT. COLEMAN

Acknowledged in Essex County Court ye 10th day of Aprill 1700 and truely recorded

pp. 33-34 THIS INDENTURE made ye Fifteenth day of January Anno Dom: 1699 Between WILLIAM STONE of ye County of RICHMOND of ye one part & FRANCIS MERIWETHER of ye County of Essex of ye other part. Witnesseth that ye sd WILLIAM STONE for Twenty pounds Ten shillings lawfull money of England to him in hand paid hath sold unto ye sd FRANCIS MERIWETHER his heires & assignes all that tract of

land containing Two hundred & fifty acres scituate in ye abovesd. County of Essex & Parish of Farnham, bounded as followeth, vizt. bounden on ye South side of HOSKINS CREEKE & then runing & bounden on JNO. MOODEY line & thence runing & bounden on JOHN GATWOODs line, & thence runing & bounden on THO: WHEELERs line & lastly bounden on MARY GREGORYs line all wch: before bargained land was sold and conveyed to ye sd WM. STONE by RICHARD GREGORY of ye sd Pish. & County of RAPPA: (now Essex County), Planter, by Deed undr: his hand & seale bearing date ye 14th day of Febry. 1679/80 & acknowledged in ye Court of ye sd RAPPA: County ye 7th day of Aprill 1680 as may appeare more fully by ye record in ye sd Court and all woods timber & trees growing all water profits & hereditaments to ye sd land belonging To have & to hold unto ye sd FRANCIS MERIWETHER his heires & assignes at all times forever hereafter peaceably hold all ye sd land wthout trouble of ye sd WM. STONE & SARAH his now Wife do by herselfe or Attorney relinquish her right of Dower to ye sd land In Wittness whereof ye sd parties to these pr:sents have sett their hands & seales
Signed sealed & delivered in ye pr:sence of us

JNO: + PENN, WILLIAM STONE
JNO: MERRITT
ANN: BURNIT

The within Deed of Sale was acknowledged by ye within named WM. STONE in Essex County Court ye 10th day of Aprill 1700 & ye right of Dower (of & to ye within menconed land) of SARAH STONE relinquished by JNO. PEATLE according to a power from ye said SARAH STONE and truely recorded. FRANCIS MERIWETHER, Cl Cur

RICHMOND County ss. I doe hereby authorize & impower you to appeare for me att ye next Court to be held for ye County of Essex for me to relinquish all my right to land sold by my Husband, WM. STONE, unto FRA: MERIWETHER of County of Essex by Deed bearing date ye fifteenth day of Janry: 1699 to be done as effectual as if I had been personally pr:sent. In Wittness whereof I have hereunto sett my hand & seale this 9th day of Aprill 1700
To JNO. PEATLE in Essex County SARAH S STONE
These truely recorded

p. 34 Essex County 1699. The Estate of WARWICK GRAY is Dr:
To my Ordr: of Cort., To ED: CRIMSHAW p Ordr., To JNO: HUDSON p Ordr., To Mr. BOUGHAN p Ordr., To JAMES BOWLER, To GEO: LOYD p Ordr., To Mr. GRIGSON p Ordr., to J: BATTAILE per Cont. by ye Inventory of ye sd Estate 5114 Total Cr: 5480

In Obedience to ye Command of ye Worppll. Court of Essex County we ye Subscribers haveinge examined ye above account & find ye Exr. of ye above sd WARWICK GRAY hath over paid Three hundred sixty & six pounds THO: HUCKLESCOTT
JNO: PEATLE

Aprill ye 11th 1700. Truely recorded according to Ordr: of Ess: County Court ye 11th of Aprill 1700. Test FRANCIS MERIWETHER, Cl Cur

p. 34 IN THE NAME OF GOD Amen. this twelfth day of Jan: 1699 I ALENER MERIT being sick & weak of body but of sound & perfect memory blessed & praised by Almighty God for ye same, do make & ordaine this to be my last Will & Testament in manner & form following; First & principally I commend my Soul into ye hands of the Almighty yt: gave it hopeing by ye Meritorious death & passion of my blessed Lord & Saviour Jesus Christ to receive a full pardon & remission of all my Sins & my body to ye ground & as for my worldly goods yt: God hath set mee, I dispose of in manner & form following

It is my last Will & Testament yt: all ye Cattle & all ye hoggs yt: I have I do leave unto my Son, JNO. MERRIT, & also ye great Table & ye pottraks & ye Spit i& ye two (? Mayors) & I doe make my Son, JOHN MERRIT, Exer. of this my last Will & Testament hereby revocking all Wills testaments legacies by me at any time made given or bequeathed & as for ye rest of ye Estate to be equally devided between my Son JNO: MERRETT & my Son, THO: MERRETT. In Wittness whereof I have hereunto sett my hand ye day above written

Test GEORGE LOYD ALENER MERRITT

JOHANNAH LOYD her marke

Proved in Essex County Court ye 11th day of Aprill 1700 by ye oathes of ye wittnesses thereto Truely recorded Test FRANCIS MERIWETHER, Cl Cur

KNOW ALL MEN by these pr:sents that we JNO. MERRIOTT & THO: MERRIOTT of ye County of Essex are bound unto JNO: CATLETT, Gent., President of ye County Court in ye sume of Forty pounds Sterling money we bind ourselves Wittness our hands this 11th day of Aprill 1700

The Condition of this obligacon is if ye above bound JNO. MERRIOTT who at a Court held for Essex County ye day & yeare abovesd. obtained a probate of ye last Will of ELLINR: MERRIOTT deceased shall at all times fullfill ye sd Will, Then this above obligacon to be woid otherwise to remain in full force

Signed sealed & delivered in ye pr:sence of us

THO: GREGSON, JNO: MERRIOTT

FRA: MERIWETHER THO: T MERRIOTT

Truely recorded Test FRANCIS MERIWETHER, Cl Cur

pp. A True and Perfect Inventory of ye Estate of Mr. GEORGE HASLEWOOD deceased
34- lying in ye County of Essex & taken & apprised this 28th of August 1693 by ye
35 Subscribers as followeth, vizt. At ye Upper Qtrs.

Imprimis To two cowes, three yerlens, three canens, one bull, one puter flagon, one brace candlestick, three cows, fore steares six yeares old and 1 seven; two bulls, one yearling, nine cowes & five calves, three heifers, three yearlings, two stears, 1 six year old ye other three; two bulls, two old bed & furniture, one English hand JOSEF LORYGHT, one Negro man Gye, two old guns, a parsell of old puter, three wedges, two old pales, three iron potts & two fryin pans & spit & one pott rack & one pestell, one pare of belloss, one pare of stilliards Total 20410

In Obedience to an Ordr: of Essex County Court baring date ye 10th day of August 1693, We ye Subscribers have appraised ye Estate of Mr. GEORGE HASLEWOOD deced in full dated this 28th day of August 1693

The Appraisers sworn August ye 26th 1693 ROBT. KAY
before me JNO: CATLETT ANDREW HERRISON
JNO: I GOOSS
JNO: PROSSER

Truely recorded Test FRANCIS MERIWETHR, Cl Cur

At a Court held for Essex County ye 11th day of Sept: 1699

Present his Majties: Justices of ye Peace

Its ordered yt: WM. TOMLIN & ANN his Wife, Admrs. of GEORGE HASLEWOOD deced render a full acct. of ye sd deced Estate in this County wch: have come to their hands as also ye Crop of Tobo: made ye yeare of ye sd HASLEWOODs death, & its ordered yt: ROBT. KAY, ANDREW HARRISON, JNO. PROSSER & REES EVANS or any three of them being summoned by ye Sheriff of this County or his Deputy some time between this & ye next Court goe to JNO: CATLETT Gent., one of his Majties. Justices of ye Peace for this County, & being before him sworne, Inventory & appraise ye Estate of ye sd deced not yet appraised & that ye sd TOMLIN & ANN his Wife return ye same together wth: ye other Appraismt. to ye next Court upon Oath

Vera Copia Test FRANCIS MERIWETHER, Cl Cur

At a Court held for Essex County ye 11th day of Novembr: 1699

Present: his Majties: Justices of ye Peace

Its ordered yt. ye last Court Order granted for Appraismt. of ye Estate of GEORGE HASLEWOOD deced not ye appraised be continued to be done some time between this & ye next Court Copia Vera Test FRANCIS MERIWETHER, Cl Cur

Essex County 9:br 23:d 1699. being sworn before Capt. JNO. CATLETT in Obedience to ye within Ordr: we ye subscribers have vallued one Negro boy wch: was all ye Estate of GEORGE HASLEWOOD wch: Mr. WM. TOMLIN did bring before us which we have valued to fore thousand Six hundred pounds of tobo: according to ye best of or: Judgment.

p me ROBT. MOSELEY, Sub Sheriff of Essex County REES EVANS
ROBT. KAY

Truely recorded Test FRANCIS MERIWETHER, Cl Cur

p. 35 KNOW ALL MEN yt: wee WM. TOMLIN & THO: GREGSON of ye County of Essex are bound unto JNO: CATLETT Gent., President of ye sd County Court, in ye sum of One hundred pound Sterling money of England to ye payment we bind ourselves this 11th: day of Aprill 1700

The Condition of this obligation is yt: if ye above bounden WM. TOMLIN, Admr. of all ye goods & credits of HANNAH TOMLIN deced, do make a true Inventory of all ye goods chattells & credits of ye sd deced & ye same so made do exhibit next County Court that shall be held and make a true & just acct. of his Administration when lawfully required & pay unto such p:sons as ye County Court shall appoint, Then this obligation to be void or else to remain in full power

Signed Sealed & delviered in pr:sence of

SALVATOR MUSCOE WILLIAM TOMLIN
THO: GREGSON

Truely recorded Test FRANCIS MERIWETHER, Cl Cur

p. 35 KNOW ALL MEN yt: wee BENJ: MOSELEY, THO: GREGSON & WM: TOMLIN of ye County of Essex are bound unto JNO: CATLETT, Gent., President of ye sd County Court in ye sum of Six hundred pounds Sterling to ye payment we bind ourselves this 11th day of Aprill 1700

The Condition of this obligation is yt: if ye above bounden BENJ: MOSELEY, Admr. with ye Will annexed of all ye chattells & credits of WM. MOSELEY, deced, during ye minority of WM. MOSELEY, Exr. therein named, do make a true Inventory of all ye goods & credits of ye sd deced & do exhibit to ye next Court held for ye above sd County of Essex & make Oath thereto & do make a true & just acct. of his Administration when he shall be lawfully required & pay unto such p:sons respectively as ye sd Court shall appoint, Then this obligation to be void or else to remain in force

Signed sealed & delivered in ye pr:sence of us

JNO: PEATLE, BENJA: MOSELEY
ROBT. MOSELEY THO: GREGSON
WILLIAM TOMLIN

Truely recorded Test FRANCIS MERIWETHER, Cl Cur

pp. 35-36 Essex County ss. This day JNO: SORELL made Complt. yt. JNO. TWIGGER stands indebted to him by Bill Six hundred & fifty six pounds of Tobo: & cask by Bill & he ye sd TWIGGR; hath lately absented himselfe out of ye County, these are therefor in his Majties. name to will & require you to attach soe much of ye Estate of ye sd JNO; TWIGGR: as wilbe of value sufficient to satisfy ye sd Debt., wth: costs & soe to provide yt: itt may be lyable to satisfy ye same hereof faile not given undr: my hand this 11th: day of Novembr: 1699

To ye High Sheriff of Essex County or his Deputy to Execute & make rept. ROBT: BROOKE

Novembr: ye 14th 1699 Then attached by vertue of ye wthin Writt one crosscut Saw, one ould bed, boulster rugg & a pr. of shoes, one small ould cattaile couch bed, 1 course sheet & coverlid, 1 ould cart wheels & cart sadle

p me JNO. TALIAFERRO, Sheriff of Essex County

p. 36 Essex County. Complaint being this day made to me by EDW: DANLIN that JNO. TWIGGER is indebted to him by Bill two thousand One hundred & fifty six pounds of tobo: & by acct Three hundred & hath absented himselfe out of this County; These are therefore in his Majties. name to require you to attach soe much of ye sd JNO: TWIGGERs Estate as will be of valew to satisfy ye sd debt & ye same to return yt: it may be lyable for satisfaction hereof faile not given undr: my hand this 11th day of Novembr: 1699

To ye High Sher: or his Deputy to Execute & make ret: FRANCIS GOULDMAN

Decembr: ye 8th 1699: By vertue of ye within Precept I have attached four cowes & four calves belonging to ye within mentioned JNO. TWIGGER.

p me ROBT. MOSELEY, Sub Sheriff

Truely Recorded FRANCIS MERIWETHER, Cl Cur

p. 36 Aprill ye 11th 1700. Sr. Pleased to answare in my sueitt yt: is against THO: SMITH & this shall be your suffician warran of Attorney from your frind and Servant to end

To Mr. HENRY GOARE These pr:sent WILLM. PART

Octobr: ye 5th 1699. Mr. THO: GREGSON pray sue THO: SMITH in my behalfe to answer for me if he does not pay you as soon as you gitt Judgmt. wth: cost sarve execution on his body & shall see you satisfied wch: is all from yor: frind to comand

Sr. Pray let ye Judgmt. pass according to ye Owner of ye Bill or else it may be paid in convenient JAMES CURTIS

January 22d: 1699 JNO: PEATLE I hereby request you to appeare for me as my Attorney in an accon depending between me & RANDLE BIRD & for your soe doing this shall be yor: sufficient warrant from yor: frind WILLIAM WILLISON

Aprill ye 10th: 1700 JOHN BALLE I request you to appear as my Attorney in accon depending in County Court of Essex upon my Acct. & for yor: soe doing this shall be yor: sufficient warrant from yor: frind DAVID GWYN

Truely recorded FRANCIS MERIWETHER, Cl Cur

p. 36 KNOW ALL MEN by these pr:sents that we JAMES BOUGHAN, JNO. BATTAILE & FRANCIS GOULDMAN of ye County of Essex, Gent., are firmly bound unto Or: Soveraigne Lord King William in ye sume of One hundred thousand pds. of Marchant tobacco & caske we bind ourselves this 10th day of Maii 1700

The Condition of this obligation is yt: whereas ye above bound JAMES BOUGHAN is by Commission appointed Sheriff of Essex County dureing his Majties. pleasure Now if sd JAMES BOUGHAN shall truely & faithfully by himselfe or such officer as shall be nominated & thereunto sworne execute all warrants proclamations & precepts wch:

shall come to him or them from his Excellency & Councell ye Genl. & Commander in Chiefe or any of yr Councell & Dilligently find out ye true quantity of land hald in ye abovesd. County by any p:sons wt:soever & return a true list or Rent Roll of ye same unto Mr. Audit: BIRD upon Oath, or such others as shall be appointed & place as he or they shall appoint & also rendr: unto him or them a p:ticular perfect acct. of all his Majties: Revenues & dues in ye sd County dureing ye time of his Sherivalty & also yt: he shall make due paymt. of all such publick dues as shall be leavied in ye aforesd. County of Essex unto ye severall persons yt: shall be appointed to receive ye same & doe performe all such things as belong to ye Office of Sheriff in ye sd County, then ye above obligation to be void or otherwise to be and remain of full force & vertue
Signed sealed & delivered in ye presence of us

HENRY GOARE, — JAMES BOUGHAN
SALVATORE MUSCOE — JNO: BATTAILE
FRA: GOULDMAN

Truely recorded Test FRANCIS MERIWETHER, Cl Cur

p. 36 IN THE NAME OF GOD Amen, the 23d day of Decembr: 1697 I DANIELL WHITEHORNE being sick & weak in body but of sound & perfict memory praise be given to God for ye same & knowing ye uncertainty of this Life on Earth & being desireous to settle things in ordr: do make this my last Will & Testament in manner & form following yt: is to say, first & principally I commend my Soul to Almighty God my Creator assuredly believing yt: I shall receive full pardon & free remission of all my Sins & be saved by ye precious death & merits of my blessed Saviour & redeemer, Christ Jesus, & my body to ye Earth from whenct. it was taken to be buried in such decent & Christian manner as to my Exex. hereafter named shall be thought meet & convenient & as touching such worldly Estate as ye Lord in mercy hath lent mee my will & meaning is ye same shall be imployed & bestowed as hereafter by this my Will is expressed & first I do renownce frustrate & make void all Wills by me formerly made & declare & appoint this my last Will & Testament

Item I give and bequeath unto JAMES CROSWEL ye Son of WM. CROSWEL fifty acres of land at ye Norwestend of my my land & further I give him all ye Estate that was his Fathers wch: may by Inventory appeare

Item I give & bequeath unto my beloved Wife, ANN WHITEHORNE, my my just debts are payed all ye rest of my Estate land goods & chattles & further I do constitute & ordaine my beloved Wife, ANN WHITEHORNE my true & lawfull Extrix. of this my last Will & Testamt. As Wittnes my hand & seale ye day & year above written
Signed & sealed in ye pr:sence of us

BRYAN NEELL, — DANIELL WHITEHORNE
EDMOND (mark) REYLEY
ELIZA: PRISE

Prov'd by the Oaths of BRYAN NEAL & EDMD. REYLEY in Essex County Court the 10th day of May 1700
Truely recorded Test FRANCIS MERIWETHER, Cl Cur

p. 37 KNOW ALL MEN by these pr:sents that we ANN WHITEHORNE, HENRY WOODNUTT & WM. HUDSON of ye County of Essex are firmly bound unto JNO. CATLETT, Gent. President of ye sd County Court in ye sum of Two hundred pds. Sterling we bind ourselves this 10th day of May 1700

The Condition of this obligation is that if ANN WHITEHORNE who at a Court held for Essex County ye day & yeare abovesd. obtained a probate of ye last Will of DANLL.

WHITEHORNE deced doe pay all Legaties & doe p:form all ye Law injoyns in such cases Then the above obligation to be void othr: wise to stand in full force
Signed sealed & delivered in pr:sence of us
HENRY GOARE — ANN (mark) WHITEHORNE
THO: GREGSON — HENRY (mark) WOODNUTT
WILLIAM (mark) HUTSON

Truely recorded Test FRANCIS MERIWETHER, Cl Cur

p. 37 THIS INDENTURE made ye 9th day of 9ber 1699 Between ROBT. DAVIES of CARNAVAN SHIRE aged about twenty one yeares of one part & LEWIS JENKINS of LEVERPOOLE of ye other part Wittnesseth yt. the sd ROBT. DAVIES doth agree from ye day of ye date hereof until ye first & next arrivall at Virginia or MARYLAND & after for & dureing ye terme of six yeares to serve in such service as ye sd LEWIS JENKINS shall there employ him in according to ye Custome of ye Country, In Consideration of ye sd, LEWIS JENKINS doth grant to pay his passage & to find & allow him meat drink apparrel & lodging wth: the othr: necessaries according to ye Custom of ye Country In Wittness whereof ye parties have sett their hands & sealed
Sealed & delivered in pr:sence of
CUTH: SHARPLE, Mayor de Leverpoole — ROBT. (mark) DAVIES
JNO: LANDFORD

Adjudged good and truely recorded according to Order of this Essex County Court 10th day of May 1700. Test FRANCIS MERIWETHER, Cl Cur

I do hereby assigne ROBT. DAVIES my Servant within mentioned unto ALICE (blot) her heirs & admrs. & assignes for ye space of six years being ye terme within mentioned from our first arrivall in Virgnia being ye 14th of Febry: 1699/1700 In Wittness whereof I ADAM OLDFORLD in ye behalfe of ye within mentioned LEWIS JENKINS do hereunto put my hand this 20th day of March 1699/1700
Wittness pr:sent ANN X BROCK her marke — ADAM OLDFIELD
May 7th: 9br: 1700 ye above assignmt. I confirme in wittness my hand
LEWIS JENKINS

Truely recorded Test FRANCIS MERIWETHER, Cl Cur

p. 37 KNOW ALL MEN by these presents that wee FRANCIS SLAUGHTER of ye County of RICHMOND and MARGUERIETT SLAUGHTER ye true & lawfull Wife of ye sd FRA: SLAUGHTER for Six thousand pounds of tobo: & caske well & truely to be paid in two Obligations bearing date wth: these presents have sold unto Mr. WM. BENDERY of ye County of Essex his heires & assignes all our right of a p:cell of land containing Two hundred twenty two acres being in ye County of Essex on ye South side of Rappahannock River & in ye freshes thereof it being part of Six hundred fifty acres of land formerly granted unto Mr. WM. FOGG & purchased by me ye sd SLAUGHTER of JNO. POWELL as by ye conveyance undr: his hand dated May ye 28th: 1679 may appeare, ye sd land to have & to hold wth: all houses & buildings fences orchards woods to ye sd land belonging from ye sd FRA: SLAUGHTER & MARGT. our heirs to ye sd Mr. WM. BENDERY his heirs or assignes without any lawfull trouble of them their heirs or assignes upon ye true & firm full payment yt. ye aforesd. Six thousand pounds of tobo: & cask according to ye fore mentioned obligation & do oblige ourselves to make an acknowledgmt. of ye sale of ye aforesd. land in ye County Court of Essex when they are required by ye sd WM. BENDERY his heirs or assignes As Wittness our hands & seales ye Twentith day of Novembr: 1699

Signed sealed & delivered in ye presence of us
NICHOLAS MORCAN, SAMUELL HENSHAW, FRA: SLAUGHTER
ISAAC FLOWER, SEM: COXE MARGARETT SLAUGHTER

Acknowledged by FRA: SLAUGHTER as also right of third acknowledged by MARGT. his Wife by ALEXR: SPENCE, her Attorney, in Essex County Court ye 10th day of May 1700 & truely recorded

I doe hereby authorize & impower Mr. ALEX: SPENCE my true & lawfull Attorney for me & in my name to acknowledge my thirds of a tract of land containing Two hundred twenty two acres unto WM: BENDREY & doe ratifie ye same as if my selfe were p:sonally pr:sent. Wittness my hand & seale this 10th of May 1700

Signed & sealed in ye pr:sence of
GEORGE MILBOURNE, MARGARETT SLAUGHTER
WM. MARSHALL

Truely recorded Test FRANCIS MERIWETHER, Cl Cur

p. 37 KNOW ALL MEN that wee WM. NORTH, WM. TOMLIN & THO: HUCKLESCOTT of ye County of Essex are held & firmly bound unto JNO: CATLETT Gent., President of ye County Court in ye sume of Two hundred pds. Sterling money of England we bind ourselves this 10th day of May 1700

The Condition of this obligation is if ye above bound WM. NORTH who at a Court held for Essex County ye day & yeare abovesd. obtained a probate of ye Last Will of ANTHO: NORTH deced doe fullfill ye sd: Will fully pay & satisfie all such Legaties as therein expressed & p:form all ye Law injoynes in such cases Then ye above obligation to be void otherwise to stand in full force

Signed sealed & delivered in ye pr:sence of us
HENRY GOARE WM: NORTH
JNO: PARKER WILLIAM TOMLIN
THO: HUCKLESCOTT

Truely recorded Test FRANCIS MERIWETHER, Cl Cur

p. 38 TO ALL TO WHOM these pr:sents shall come I JOHN WOOD of ye Parish of Cittenborne in ye County of Essex within ye Colony of Virginia, Planter, send greeting Now Know ye that I ye sd. JOHN WOOD as well for ye good will love & affection wch: I have unto my loveing Grandchild, JNO: WOOD, Sonne of HENRY WOOD deced, as alsoe for divers other considerations hath given unto him ye sd JNO: WOOD all that parcell of land being in ye Parish & County aforesd. containing One hundred & seventy acres wch: sd. tract of land I purchased of ROBERT & THOMAS MOSS as by Assignment of a Deed of Sale bearing date ye 11th day of July 1674; And also twenty & nine acres of land more granted to me by Patent bearing date ye 3d day of Octobr: 1690, adjoyning to ye aforesd. One hundred & seventy acres wch: sd. Conveyance & Patten together containes One hundred Ninety & nine acres bounded as will appear by ye aforesd. Conveyance & Patent relation being had together wth: all appurtenances & alsoe all ye Estate, right to ye same which sd tracts or parcells of land are now in ye occupation of CASANDER WOOD, Widow, and Mother of ye sd JOHN WOOD, To have & to hold ye sd parcells of land wth: all houses orchards gardens & other ye premisses unto ye sd JNO. WOOD & ye heirs of his body lawfully to be begotten for ever And if it soe happen ye sd JNO. WOOD dye without issue then I give ye aforesd. land to his Brother, HENRY WOOD, & his heirs lawfully to be begotten forever & if ye sd HENRY should dye without such lawfull heir then to ELIZ: WOOD, Sister of ye sd JOHN & HENRY WOOD and her heirs lawfully begotten for ever, And if it happen that ye sd ELIZ: WOOD should dye without such lawfull heir as

aforesd. then after ye decease of CASANDER WOOD (Mother of ye aforesd. JOHN, HENRY & ELIZA.) I give ye aforesd. land unto my Sonne, THOMAS WOOD, & his heirs lawfully to be begotten And ye said JNO: WOOD for himselfe and his heirs ye sd parcell of land hereby granted & sold wth: the appurtenances unto ye sd JNO: WOOD his heirs & assignes and ye heirs of his body lawfully to be begotten forever against him ye sd JNO: WOOD and all other p:sons wt:soever claiming under him In Wittness whereof ye sd JOHN WOOD, Grand Father of ye above named JOHN, HENRY & ELIZABETH WOOD, hath hereunto sett his hand and affixed his seale ye 10th day of May 1700
Signed sealed & delivered in ye presence of us

JOHN PEATLE, JOHN W WOOD
THOMAS MUNDAY
JOHN J SPIRES

Acknowledged in Essex County Court ye 10th day of May 1700 truely recorded

p. 38 THIS INDENTURE made this Ninth day of May in ye yeare of or: Lord God One thousand seven hundred Between GEORGE LOYD of ye County of Essex together wth: JOANNA his Wife within ye Colony of Virginia, Planter, of ye one part, & JOHN, MARY & DANIEL DISKINS, Sonns & Daughter of DANIEL DISKINS late of ye Pish of Cittenbourn in ye County aforesd. Planter, deced of ye other part Wittnesseth that for & in consideration of a Legatie given by ye sd DANIEL DISKINS unto his sd: Sonnes & Daughter and by him ordeined to purchase land for his sd: Sonnes & Daughter, as by relation had to ye last Will & Testament of ye aforesd. DANIEL DISKINS may more at large appear, he ye sd. GEORGE LOYD hath sold & confirmed to ye sd: JOHN, MARY & DANIEL DISKINS their heirs & assignes all that tract of land containing Three hundred acres being in Parish of St. Maries & County of Essex ye sd: Three hundred acres being ye uppermost part of a certain dividend of land sold unto ye sd GEORGE LOYD by THOMAS MEADOWS of ye County of Essex, Planter, & mentioned in an Indenture undr: ye hand & seale of ye sd: THOMAS MEADOWS baring date ye Tenth day of August One thousand six hundred Ninty & nine wth: all & singular Houses tobacco houses orchards gardens timber profitts and appurtenances wt:soever to ye sd three hundred acres of land & all deeds Patents wt:soever touching any part of them To have & to hold ye sd land & all & singular ye pr:misses unto ye sd JOHN, MARY & DANIEL DISKINS their heirs & assignes forever paying ye Rent & performeing ye services wch: shall hereafter become due for & in respect of ye pr:misses aforesd., unto or: Sovereign Lord ye King, And ye sd GEORGE LOYD & JOANNA his Wife for themselves & their heirs ye sd land against him & every other persons wt:soever will warrant & for ever defend & at all times hereafter quietly enter into occupie & enjoy all & singular the before hereby granted p:misses without any trouble of ye sd GEORGE LOYD & JOANNA his Wife their heirs or any other persons wt:soever In Wittness whereof ye parties first above named have sett their hands & seales
Signed sealed & delivered in ye p:sence of us

JAMES BOUGHAN, GEORGE LOYDE
ROBERT COLEMAN JOANNA I LOID
THOMAS HUCKLESCOTT

Acknowledged & right of Dower relinquished in Essex County Court ye 10th day of May 1700 truely recorded Test FRANCIS MERIWETHER, Cl Cur

pp. 39-40 THIS INDENTURE made this fourth day of Aprill One thousand seven hundred and in the Twelfth yeare of or: Sovereigne Lord William the Third over England Scotland France Ireland and Virginia, King &c., Betweene ROBT. HAMILTON, Sonne & heire of LUKE HAMILTON deceased, of ye one part and THOMAS

TOMLINNE of ye other part Wittnesseth that ye sd ROBERT HAMILTON for a valuable consideration have sold unto THOMAS TOMLINNE his heirs and assignes for ever all his right of certain parcell of land conteining Two hundred acres of land being in ye County of Essex on ye South side of HOSKINS Poqoson beginning at ye Poquoson side upon ELECK ROBINs line and runing for length into the woods, ye sd land being sold unto ye abovesd. LUKE HAMILTON & JAMES HARPER by Capt. THOMAS GOULDMAN late of ye County of RAPPAHANNOCK deced as by an Instrument of Writeing bearing date the 2 day of January 1674/5, & acknowledged in ye sd Court ye 5th day of ye same moneth & yeare may appeare, And by right of Inheritance becoming due to ye sd ROBERT HAMILTON, To have and to hold the sd land with all woods water & appurtenances thereunto belonging to ye sd THOMAS TOMLINNE his heirs and assignes subject never ye less to the quit rents that shall grow due to our Sovereign Lord ye King, And ye sd ROBERT HAMILTON for ye sd valuable consideration will defend unto ye sd THOMAS TOMLINNE his heirs & assignes from him or from any other persons under him & due acknowledgment make of all the before mentioned sold land before the Justices hold Court for ye County of Essex and there to be recorded according to ye Statute in that case provided In Wittness whereof ye sd ROBERT HAMILTON hath sett his hand & fixed his seale
Signed sealed & delivered in presence of us

WILLIAM ALLEN — ROBERT HAMIL H TON
THOMAS HUCKLESCOTT — his marke

Acknowledged in Essex County Court ye 10th day of May 1700 & truely recorded

KNOW ALL MEN that wee ROBERT HAMILTON and ELIZABETH BRUTNELL are bound unto THOMAS TOMMLINNE his heirs and assignes in ye full summe of Three thousand pounds of good sound merchantable tobaccoe & caske convenient to a landing in Essex Countye we bind ourselves this 4th day of Aprill in ye yeare of our Lord One thousand seven hundred & in ye twelfth yeare of the Reigne of our Sovereign Lord William ye third &c.

The Condition of this obligation is that if ye above bounded ROBERT HAMILTON do well & sufficiently defend unto ye above mentioned THOMAS TOMLINNE his heirs a certain parcell of land mentioned in an Instrument of Writeing bearing date wth: these pr:sents from him ye sd ROBT: HAMILTON his heirs and assignes or any other person under him laying claime for ye same, That then this obligation to be voide or else to remain in full power
Signed sealed and delviered in the presence of us

WILLIAM ALLEN, — ROBERT HAMIL H TON,
THOMAS HUCKLESCOTT — ELIZABETH BRUTNELL E her marke

Acknwledged in Essex County Court ye 10th day of May 1700 & truely recorded

p. 40 KNOW ALL MEN by these pr:sents that wee ROBT: MOSS, THOMAS DAVIS & HENRY NEWTON of ye County of Essex are firmly bound unto JNO: CATLETT Gent., President of ye County Court in ye sum of Fifty pounds sterling money of England we bind ourselves 10th day of May 1700

The Condition of this obligation is that if ye above bounded ROBT. MOSS, Admr. of all & singular ye goods chattells & credits of REBECA MOSS deced do make Inventory of all ye goods & credits of ye sd deced wch: shall come to his possession & ye same do exhibit to ye next Court & make oath thereto & further do make a just account when he shall be thereunto lawfully required & all ye rest wch: shall be found remaineing upon ye sd Admr. shall deliver & pay unto such persons respectively as pursuant to Law shall appoint, Then this obligation to be void otherwise to stand in full power

Signed sealed & delivered in pr:sence of us

HENRY GOARE, ROBT. MOSS
THOMAS WINSLOW HENRY NUTON
THOMAS DAVIS

Truely recorded Test FRANCIS MERIWETHER, Cl Cur

p. 40 TO ALL TO WHOM these pr:sents shall come Greeting. Whereas their Majties. King William & Queen Mary by their Royal Charter bearing date at Westminster ye Eighth day of Febry: in ye fourth yeare of their Reigne graciously pleased to give unto FRANCIS NICHOLAON, Lt. & Governor of Virginia & MARYLAND, WILLIAM COLE, RALPH WORMELEY, WILLIAM BYRD & JOHN LEAR Esqr., JAMES BLAIR, JOHN HARINFOLDD, STEPHEN FENACE & SAMLL. GRAY, Clerks, THOMAS MILNER, CHRISTOPHER ROBINSON, CHARLES SCARBURGH, JOHN SMITH, BENJAMIN HARRISON, MILES CARY, HENRY HARTWELL, WILLIAM RANDOLPH & MATHEW PAGE, Gent., Trustees for ye COLLEDGE of WILLIAM & MARY & ye longest livers or longest liver of them ye Office of Surveyr: Genll. of their sd Colony of Virginia to be had & executed with all its fees profits advantages liberties & preferments by then ye sd Trustees or by such Officers & Substitutes as they or ye majr. part of them shall appoint untill ye sd COLLEDGE shall be actually founded & erected as by ye sd Charter (relation being thereunto had) may appear & whereas ye Survivors of ye sd Trustees have by their Comission under their hands & seale of ye COLLEDGE dated ye 25th day of Febry: in ye Eleventh year of his Majties: reign contituted me, MILES CARY, Surveyr: Genll. in their name to execute ye sd Office of Surveyor Genll., I ye sd MILES CARY out of ye good confidence & certain knowledge I have of integrity of CHARLES SMITH to execute ye Office of Surveyr: have nominted & apoint him ye sd CHARLES SMITH to be Surveyr: of all ye lands in County of RICHMOND & that part of Essex ( ) by Coll. MOSELEY with full power & authority to him to measure & lay out any parcell of land within ye sd County. I do further give him power to ask demand & receive all such fees profits as now are or hereafter shall be due by ye Lawes of this Country paying unto ye above mentioned Trustees or ye longest liver of them for ye use of ye sd COLLEDGE one full sixth part of all ye yearly profits that shall come to him as ye sd Surveyors hath ( ) of his Commission to ye abovesd. Trustees or their order at such time & place as they from time to time shall appoint this Comission to continue dureing pleasure of ye sd Trustees Given under my hand & seale this 4th day of May 1700

MILES CARY Surveyr: Genll.

Truely recorded according to Order of Essex County Court ye 10th day of May 1700

p. 40 Capt. THO: GRIGSON I doe impower you by vertue of a Letter of Attorney I have from GRACE SWEATMAN to apeare in my name to gett for her Letters of Administration on her deceast Husbands Estate & to prosecute all actions I may or she might have thereby eyther for her interest or my one in any actions for eyther of us may hereafter be had or brought in Essex County against any manner of person & doe give you ye power I my selfe have or might have in or about ye pr:misses in what you shall lawfully doe. Wittness my name & seale this 7th of May 1700

RICH: COVINGTON RICH: WILLIS
LEO: HILL

Prov'd in Essex County Court ye 10th day of May 1700 by ye oathes of ye wittnesses hereto & truely recorded Test FRANCIS MERIWETHER, Cl Cur

p. 40 KNOW ALL MEN by these pr:sents yt: we WM. AYRES, EDWD. GOULDMAN & THOMAS THORPE of ye County of Essex are firmly bound unto JNO. CATLETT Gent., Presedent of ye County Court in ye sum of One hundred pds. Sterling we bind our selves this 11th day of May 1700

The Condition of this obligacon is that if ye above bounded WM. AYRES & ANN his Wife, Admr: debonis non administratis of all ye goods & credits of Capt. ANTHONY SMITH deced do make a true & perfect Inventory of all goods & credits of ye sd deced & ye same do exhibit to ye next Court that shall be held for ye abovesd. County of Essex & make oath thereto & truely admr. according to Law & further do make true & just acct. of their administration when required & residue of ye sd goods pay unto such p:sons respectively as ye Court p:suant to Law shall appoint, Then this obligacon to be void otherwise to remain in full force

Signed sealed & delivered in ye presence of us

HENRY GOARE
GARETT LYNCH

WILLIAM AYRES
EDW: GOULDMAN
THOMAS T THARPE

Truely recorded Test FRANCIS MERIWETHER, Cl Cur

pp. 40-41 KNOW ALL MEN by these pr:sents that wee FRA: GOULDMAN, EDWD. GOULDMAN, JNO: PARKER & WM. AYRES of ye County of Essex are firmly bound unto JNO. CATLETT Gent., Presedent of ye sd County Court in ye sum of One hundred pounds Sterling we bind ourselves this 17th day of May 1700

The Condition of this obligacon is that if FRA: GOULDMAN & EDWD. GOULDMAN, Admrs. of all & singular ye goods & credits of ROBT: GOULDMAN deced do make a true Inventory of all ye chattells & credits of ye sd deced & ye same so made do exhibit to ye next Court for ye County of Essex & make oath thereto & further do make a true & just acct. of their Administration when lawfully required & all ye rest pay unto such p:sons as ye sd Court shall appoint, Then this obligacon to be void otherwise to remain in full force

Signed sealed & delivered in ye pr:sence of us

THO: HUCKLESCOTT,
HEN: GOARE

FRANCIS GOULDMAN
EDWARD GOLDMAN
JOHN PARKER
WILLIAM AYRES

Truely recorded Test FRANCIS MERIWETHER, Cl Cur

p. 41 KNOW ALL MEN that wee JNO: WEBSTER, JAMES BOUGHAN & RICHD. COVINGTON of ye County of Essex are bound unto JNO: CATLETT Gent., President of ye sd County Court in ye sum of Twenty four thousand pds. of tobo: & caske we bind ourselves this 10th day of May 1700

The Condition of this obligacon is that if JNO. WEBSTER, Guardian of WM. SMITH, Orphan of ANTHO: SMITH deced, his heirs truely pay unto ye sd Orphan all such estate as come to ye hands of ye sd JNO: WEBSTER as soon as ye sd Orphan shall come to lawfull age or when required by ye Justices of ye Peace for Essex County Court as also to keep harmless ye sd Justices from all damages about ye sd Estate, ye above obligacon to be void otherwise to remain in full power

Signed sealed & delivered in ye pr:sence of us

THO: GREGSON,
FRANCIS MERIWETHER

JOHN WEBSTER
JAMES BOUGHAN
RICHD: COVINGTON

Truely recorded Test FRANCIS MERIWETHER, Cl Cur

p. 41 May ye 10th 1700. I doe hereby authorise & impower you JNO. BATTAILE to appear for me in Essex Court to defend all such actions as shall bee there depending betwixt THO: THARPE Plt. & my selfe Deft., for wch: so doeing this shall be your warrant

To JNO: BATTAILE These from JAMES JONES

p. 41 To ye Worpl. Court of Essex County: THOMAS GREGSON prayes that the ear mark of his Cattle & hoggs & sheep by order of this Court put on Record being as followeth a crop slitt & over keel in each

Truely recorded according to Ordr. of Essex County Court ye 11th day of July 1700

p. 41 To ye Worpl. Court of Essex County, JOHN CLARKE humbly prayes that ye ear marke of his Cattle & hoggs hereunder set down may be recorded amongst ye Records of this County Court. The ear marke of JOHN CLARKE cattel & hoggs is as followeth to wit: a slitt on ye right ear & a swallow forke on ye left eare

Truely recorded according to Ordr: of Essex County Court ye 11th day of July 1700

p. 41 IN THE NAME OF GOD Amen. I JOHN ELLETT of South Farnham Pish. in ye County of Essex being very sick & weak butt of perfect sence & memory doe make this my last Will & Testament in maner & form following, this First day of July 1698.

First I give & bequeath my Soul unto Almighty God hoping for pardon of all my sins through the only meritts of my blessed Lord & Savour Jesus Christ att ye last Day; my body I give unto my Mother, ye Earth, to be desentllye & Christianly interred by my Exr. or Exec. hereafter named shall think fitt & my worlly estatt wch: God hath lent me after my just debts & funerall charges are sattisfyed I give in maner following:

2ly. I give unto my loving Wife, EALES ELLETT, my Plantacon & all my land that I am now possessed wth: all or any ways belongs to me during my sd: Wifes life wthoutt ye lett or molestation of any pr:son whatsoever & after my sd Wifes departure outt of this life then ye sd land to be my Daugher, JOANE ELLETTs, during her life & after her decease ye sd land to be my two Daughters, EALES ELLETT & FRA: ELLETT, to be equally devided both for goodness & qntity. to them & their heirs for ever

3dly. I give unto my Daughter, ELIZABETH PAINE, one Cow yeareling with all her increase for ever to her & her heres for ever & for all ye rest of my worly estate I give unto my aforesd. Loving Wife for to be att her own disposall as she shall think fitte & I doe appoynt & ordaine my Loving Wife my whole & sole Executorix of this my last Will & Testament & this to cutt of all former Wills Deeds & Giftes whatsoever As Witnesseth my hand & seale ye day & year above written

Signed sealed & delivered in the presence of

JOHN I BRAISER — JOHN | ELLETT
RICHARD R HUGINES
THO: WHEELER

Prov'd in Essex County Court the 10th day of July 1700 by the Oathes of RICHD. HUTCHINS & JNO. BRAISIER Truely recorded Test FRANCIS MERIWETHER, Cl Cur

KNOW ALL MEN by these presents that wee ALICE ELLETT, JNO: BROOKE & RICH: HUTCHINS of ye County of Essex are held & firmly bound unto JNO: CATLETT Gent., Presedent of ye sd County Court in ye summ of Twenty thousand pounds of tobo: we bind our selves wittness our hands & seales this 10th day of July 1700

The Condition of this obligacon is that if ye above bound ALICE ELLETT who in Court held for Essex County ye daye & year abovesd. obtained a Probate of ye last Will of JNO: ELLITT deced shall at all times hereafter p:form & satisfie all such Legats. as therein

expressed & wt:soever ye Law enjoyns in such cases Then ye above obligacon to be void othewise to stand in full force
Signed sealed & delivered in ye pr:sence of us

HEN: GOARE, ALIS + ELLITT
THOMAS HUCKLESCOTT JOHN BROOKS
RICHD: R HUTCHINS

Truely recorded Test FRANCIS MERIWETHER, Cl Cur

pp. 41-42 TO ALL XEN: PEOPLE to whome these pr:sents shall come Know you yt: I JAMES FUGATT late of Virga: Gent., for divers good causes but more especially for ye summ of Fifteene pounds Sterling & Five pounds to be paid to my now Wife, DOROTHEY have sould to RICHD. WYATT of KING & QUEEN County Gent. his heirs or assignes all ye parcell of land didn ye Coty: of Essex or RAPPA: & by ye Will & Testament of THO: PETTITT deced beareing date Sept: ye 20th 1663 was given to my Wife as aforesd. for wch: sd land I acknowledged my selfe fully contented & payd have demised ye sd land being by estemation Two hundred & eighty acres according to ye severall courses there of being in the Coty: aforesd., & bounded as followeth, beginning at a marked Pokokery & runing for breath up HOSKINS CREEK on ye Eastward side, thence W: by S: to a marked red Oake standing on ye Eastward side of a small branch or gutt & for length by or nigh ye side of ye sd branch S: by E:, thence E: by N: for breath againe So. N: & so N: by W: to ye place where it first began & likewise we doe make over to ye sd WYATT his heires my rite & intrest of One hundred acres of land adjoyning to ye aforesd. land as by ye aforesd. Will & Testament will more at large apeare; to wch: land & every part thereof I doe firmly make over from me my heires to ye sd WYATT his heires & will forever defend this my saile from ye claim of any p:sons wt:soever & will by my selfe or Lawfull Attorney acknowledge this my Sale in KING & QUEEN County Court when required by ye sd WYATT or any Court in Virga: to wch: I have sett my hand & Seale this 10th: day of 9ber: 1699
Signed sealed & delivered in pr:sents of us

THO: SPENCER, JAMES FUGATT
MATT: CREED

At a Court held for KING & QUEEN County May 13th 1700
ROBT. NAPIER by vertue of a Power of Attorney from JAMES FUGATT Gent. to him ye sd ROBT. appeared & acknowledged the within Deed to RICHARD WYATT Gent. & at ye sd WYATTs request was admitted to Record

Test JOHN PIGG, D. C. Con:

The within Deed of Sale was acknowledged in Essex County Court ye 10th day of July 1700 by ROBERT NAPIER, impowered therefore by JAMES FUGATT within named and is truely recorded Test FRANCIS MERIWETHER, Cl Cur

KNOW ALL MEN by these pr:sents that I JAMES FUGATT, late of Virginia, have & fully apoint Mr. ROBT. NAPIER of KING & QUEEN County my true & lawfull Attorney to acknowledge every such Deeds & powers that doe hereby relate to me or my Wife but more especially to acknowledge one Deed of Sale for land being now in ye County of Essex formerly RAPPA: wch: land comeing to me by maring DORATHE PETTIT, ye Daughter of THO: PETTIT deceased, now going by ye name of DORATHE FUGETT & what ever my sd Attorney shall doe I doe hereby ratifie in maner if I my selfe might doe if pr:sent & doe declare that I will ever dise owne DORATHE FUGETT to be my Wife being parted this Sixteen yeares past as Wittness my hand this 10th: day of 9br: 1699

Test THO: SPENCER JAMES FUGETT
MATT: CREED

At a Court held for KING & QUEEN County May 13th: 1700
The within Power of Attorney was proved by ye Oaths of THOMAS SPENCER & MATTHEW CREED Evidences thereto & admitted to Record Test JOHN PIGG, D. Cl Cur
Truely recorded Test FRANCIS MERIWETHER, Cl Cur

pp. 42-43 THIS INDENTURE made the tenth day of June 1700 Between THOMAS GREGSON of ye Pish: of Cittenbourn in ye Countye of Essex of ye one part & ERASMUS ALLEN & WILLIAM ALLEN of ye Parish of South Farnham in ye Countye of Essex aforesd., Planters, of ye other part Wittnesseth that ye sd THOMAS GREGSON Gentleman for Three thousand seven hundred pounds of good sound sweet scented tobacco hath sold unto ye sd ERASMUS ALLEN & WILLIAM ALLEN their heires & assignes all that parcell of land or Woodland Ground containing Two hundred acres being in Essex County formerly RAPPAHANNOCK County upon ye South side of Rappahannock River & bounded as followeth Beginning at a corner Oak on a hill side by a branch upon ye line of RANDEL GREGORY & thence runing North East & by East to a corner Spanish Oak on a hill side, thence East to a corner white Oak on a branch & thence along ye branch North to a corner Pine by a HORSE PATH & thence South West to an other corner Pine belinging to ye land of Coll: GOODWIN & Mr. HENRY AWBREY standing at ye head of a branch & thence down ye sd branch to ye place where it first began; And all wayes timber swamps profitts & appurtenances wt:soever all wch: sd parsell of land is part of a Divident of Nine hundred acres of land granted by Patent bearing date ye 20th of Aprill 1684 unto JAMES BOUGHAN & JOHN BOUGHAN, and by ye sd JAMES BOUGHAN sold & conveyed unto GEORGE SUCKETT & GEORGE REED by a Deed of Sale bareing date ye 13th of February 1685/6 & by ye sd GEORGE SUCKETT sold unto PETER RICHARDSON by a Deed of Sale bareing date ye 28th: of August 1689; & by EVAN RICE, Attorney of ye sd PETER RICHARDSON, sold unto JOSEPH SMITH by a Deed of Sale bearing date ye 9th day of Aprill 1694 & by ye sd JOSEPH SMITH sold unto WILLIAM DOWNING by a Deed of Sale bearing date ye 6th day of May 1696 & by ye sd WILLIAM DOWNING sold & assigned & set over unto ye sd THOMAS GREGSON by an Assignment beareing date ye 7th: of December 1696 And all rights whatsoever of him ye sd THOMAS GREGSON to ye pr:misses To have and to hold unto ye sd ERASMUS ALLEN & WILLIAM ALLEN paying the Rent & p:forming ye services which shall grow due & payable unto or: Soveraigne Lord ye King, And the said THOMAS GREGSON for himselfe and his heires ye: sd: land herby granted will for ever defend and that they by force & vertue of these pr:sents at all times hereafter lawfully & quietly enter into & enjoy ye sd land wthout any trouble or interuption of ye sd THOMAS GREGSON In Wittness whereof ye parties their hands & seales have sett
Signed sealed & delivered in ye presence of us

HEN: GOARE, THO: GREGSON
THOMAS HUCKLESCOTT

Acknowledged in Essex County Court ye 10th of July 1700 & truely recorded

p. 43 THIS INDENTURE made ye 16 day of December 1699 Between RICHARD HADDOCK of LEALAND in ye County of LANCASTER aged about Fourteen yeares on ye one part & JNO: WALLS of LEVERPOOLE in ye sd County, Navigat:, on ye other part Wittnesseth that ye sd RICHARD HADDOCK doth grant with ye sd JOHN WALLS his heires & assignes from ye day of ye date hereof unto his first & next arrivall in Virginia or MARYLAND & after and during ye terme of Eleven yeares to searve in such searvice & imploymts. as he ye sd JNO. WALLS shall there imploy him in according to ye Custome of ye Country in ye like kind, In Consideracon whereof ye sd JNO: WALLS doth hereby grant with the said RICHARD HADDOCK to pay for his passage & to allow him meat drink

apparrell lodgins with other necessaries according to ye Custome of ye Countrey In Wittness whereof ye parties have sett their hands & seales
Sealed & delivered in pr:sence of
JOHN SANDIFORD, JNO: WALLS
HAZLEWOOD
Adjudged good in Essex County Court ye 10th day of July 1700 & truely recorded

p. 43 KNOW ALL MEN by these pr:sents that I JOHN HAWKINS of ye County of Essex wth: ELIZABETH my Wife do sell to SAMUELL WORRIN & to his heires & assignes for ever Fifty acres of land being in ye County of Essex and on ye South side of Rappa: River & on ye North side of OCCUPATION RUN & begineth at a marked Maple standing by ye sd Run & thence runeth North to a Stake standing as corner tree & thence West North West to a marked Spanish Oake & thence South to ye Mayne Run of OCCUPATION to a marked Aish & finealy downe ye sd Run to ye first mentioned station, to him ye sd WORIN & to his heires To have hold & enjoy wth: warranty from me our heires to him & his heires & assignes forever without the molestation or claimes of us our heires or any pr:son wt:soever As Wittness our hands & seales this 20th day of Septembr: 1698
Signed sealed & delivered in the pr:sence of us
JEREM: PARKER, JOHN HAWKINS
JAMES J MASTERS ELIZABETH E HAWKINS
Acknowledged & right of Dower relinquished in Essex County Court ye 10th day of Novembr: 1698 & truely recorded. Test FRANCIS MERIWETHER, Cl Cur

KNOW ALL MEN by these pr:sents that I SAMLL. WARREN for and in consideration of Twelve hundred & thirtye pounds of good sound tobo: to me in hand paid do by these pr:sents sell all my right & demand of & to ye sd wthin mentioned land and conveiance unto HUGH CARYE his heires & assignes forever from my heires or from all other p:rsons wt:soever will warrant & defend unto ye sd HUGH CARYE his heires and assignes for ever In Wittness whereof I have sett my hand & seale this 28th: day of June 1700
Signed sealed & delivered in pr:sence of
THOMAS HUCKLESCOTT, SAMLL. + WARREN
WILLIAM ALLEN
Acknowledged in Essex County Court the 10th day of July 1700 & truely recorded

p. 43 An Inventory & apraismt. of ROBART BUMBARY deseed his Estate
To 4 cowes & 2 calves, 4 two yeare old, 1 mare, 1 flock bead one bolster 1 rugg, 1 feather bead bolster & rug, 8 pounds of puter, 13 yds. & a halfe of Ostenbridge, 16 yds. of Sharge, 1 old frying pan, 2 poots, 2 poothookes & rack Total 5270
These appraisers sworne before me this
20th of February 1698/9 Preaised by us JOHN WATERS
THO: EDMONDSON JOHN GAMES
LEONARD CHAMBERLINE
Decembr: ye 19th: day 1699. Then RICHARD DAY mead oyath before me that this within menconed is a true & perfect Inventory of ROBT. BUMBARYs Estate to ye beste of his knowlege given under my hand ye day yeare above written
JAMES BOUGHAN
To three Sowes & piges come to ye hands of me ye Subscriber sence this Inventory taken WILLIAM JOHNSON
Truely recorded Test FRANCIS MERIWETHER, Cl Cur

p. 43 On ye back of an Ordr: granted for ye Apprmt. of ye Estate of JNO. TWIGGER returneth attached for satisfaction of debt due to JNO: SORRELL was writ as followeth vizt., ye appraisment of ye goods attacht. by Capt. JNO. TALIAFERRO appraised inne 7br: 4th

To a Cart & wheeles 550 lbs.; to a feather bed bolster, a pr: of sheets & a coverled 650; total: 1200

Sworn before me
BER: GAINES

SAM: HENSHAW
JAMES BOULWARE
DAVID WILLSON

Truely recorded Test FRANCIS MERIWETHER, Cl Cur

p. 44 William the Third by ye grace of God &c. to JNO: CATLETT, THO: EDMONDSON, FRA: TALIAFERRO, BERNARD GAINES, ROBT. BROOKE, JNO. BATTAILE, JNO. TALIAFERRO, FRANCIS GOULDMAN, RICHD. COVINGTON, JAMES BOUGHAN, DANL. DOBYNS, ROBT. PAYNE, THO: MERIWETHER, WM. TOMLIN, BENJA: MOSELEY, SAML. THACKER & ROBT. COLEMAN Gent. greeting. Know yee that wee have assigned you Justices to keep the peace of ye County of Essex all Ordinances Statutes of our Kingdom of England & Laws of this our great Colony of Virga: made for the good of ye peace & for the quiet rule of ye people in every ye articles thereof in ye said County to chastise, punish all persons agt. ye formes of those Ordinances Statutes of our Kingdom of England and Lawes of this our Colony cause to come before you all those persons who shall threaten any of our Leige people either in their bodys or burning theire houses, to find sufficient security for the peace or for ye good behaviour and if they shall refuse then to cause them to be kept safe in prison untill they find such security, Wee have also assigned you to meet at ye usual place of holding Courts at certain dayes & determine all suits controversies & debates between party & party according to ye Lawes of the Kingdom of England & of this our Antient & great Colony & Dominion of Virga: likewise to you to take deposicons & examinacons upon all for ye better manifestacon of ye truth in all matters & keep or cause to be kept all Orders of Court directed to you from our Governr: or Comandr: in Cheife and our Councill of State and to punish ye offendrs: & breakers of the same, And further to cause the Clerk of your Court to keep Records of all Judgmts. Rules & Orders decided And further every one of you that you dilligently intend the keeping of the Peace also that at those certaine dayes & places cause to come before you or any four or more of you such good & lawfull men ye Sheriff his Bayliwick by whom the Truth in the matter may be the better known & inquired of Witness our Trusty & well beloved FRANCIS NICHOLSON Esqr. our Lt. Govr: of our Colony & Dominion of Virginia at JAMES TOWN under the seale of our Colony ye 25th day of Aprill in ye twelfth year of our Reign 1700

A Comission of the Peace for Essex County

E. JENINGS Depty: Secry: FR. NICHOLSON

Truely recorded Test FRANCIS MERIWETHER, Cl Cur

p. 45 William the third by ye grace of God &c. to JNO. CATLETT, THO: EDMONDSON, FRA: TALIAFERRO, BERNARD GAINES, ROBT. BROOKE, JNO. BATTAILE, JNO. TALIAFERRO, FRANCIS GOULDMAN, RICHD. COVINGTON, JAMES BOUGHAN, DANL. DOBYNS, ROBT. PAYNE, THO: MERIWETHER, WM. TOMLIN, BENJA: MOSELEY, SAML. THACKER & ROBT. COLEMAN Gent. greeting (A Dedimus for Administring ye Oathes & Test &c. to ye Justices of ye Peace for Essex County) ye 25th day of Aprill in ye Twelfth year of our Reign 1700

E. JENNINGS Depty. Secry: FR: NICHOLSON

Truely recorded Test FRANCIS MERIWETHER, Cl Cur

p. 45 Virga: Sct. At JAMES CITY ye 10th of July 1700 in ye 12th year of ye Reign of William the third &c. Present his Excellency in Councill

Whereas severall frauds & abuses have been comitted hereto fore in concealing County and Parish Tithes & severall guifts & donacons made to Schools and other pious uses then was by the Doners intended for detecting and preventing whereof as much as may be, His Excellency by & with ye advice of his Majties. Honble. Councill is pleased to direct & doth hereby require that all the Magistrates of each & every respective County & Counties within this his Majties. Colony & Dominion of Virginia shall at ye next Court held for each of the said Counties respectively essue out an Order directed to ye several Vestreyes of each & every Parish & Parishes within their respective Counties commanding them & each & every of them at the next Court to be held for ye said County to render unto the Justices in Court then sitting a true & just acct. of each & every Individual Tithable in each & every of their respective Parishes this present year 1700 and a true & perfect acct. Debitor Creditor of each & every their Parish levies the last year 1699 as also ye extents bounds & limitts of their several Parishes together with an acct. of what GLEBE or GLEBE LAND to each & every of them belonging of what value & estimate what Guifts & donacons for ye advancement of Schools or other pious uses when & by whom given, how improved & whose custody they now are, wch: accots. soe as aforesd. given by ye Vestry or Church Wardens of each respective Parish to ye County Court wch: they belong is by the said Court to be certified in manner & forme aforesd. and to be given to their respective BURGESSes in order to be laid before the Genll. Assembly at their next session. And his Excellcy: by & with the advice aforesd doth further direct & require ye Magistrates of each & every respective County Court or Courts within this Dominion of Virginia that they cause a true & perfect list of each & every individual Titheable in each & every their respective County & Couties this pr:sent year 1700 And also a true & perfect Accot. Debitor & Creditor of each & every their respective County Levies the last year 1699, together with an accot. of the extents bounds & limitts of each respective County to be drawn out & laid before them all wch: being so done & perfected His Excellency with the advice of his Majties. Honble: Councill is pleased to direct & doth hereby require each & every respective Court & Courts within this Colony to send downe by their severall BURGESSes in order to be laid before the Genll. Assembly at their next session. And to take off all excuse & pretensions of ignorance, it is ordered and appointed that the Sheriff of each respective County & Counties within this Colony & Dominion do cause this Order to be publick read in their several County Courts & in each & every Church & Chapell in each & every respective Parish & Parishes within their County

DIONISIES WRIGHT

Truely recorded Test FRANCIS MERIWETHER, Cl Cur

p. 45 KNOW ALL MEN that wee THOMAS MERIWETHER, ROBERT COLEMAN & FRANCIS MERIWETHER of Essex are firmly bound unto LEONARD HILL of the same County in the sum of Sixty two pounds Thirteen Shills. Stearl. to ye payment we bind ourselves Wittness our hand & seales this 11th day of 7br: 1700

The Condition of this obligation is that whereas LEO: HILL upon an accon of the Case brought to Essex County Court agt. the abovebound THOMAS MERIWETHER, Gardian to KATHR: & FRANCES WM:SON, Surviveing Exer. of the last Will & Testament of HENRY WILLIAMSON deced has at a Court held for the sd County on the 11th day of 7br: 1700 recovered Judgmt. agt. the above bound THOMAS MERIWETHER for Thirty one pds. Six Shills. & six pence Sterl., and whereas the said THO: MERIWETHER &c. has pray'd an appeale from the sd Judgmt., to ye Generall Court Councill on ye 7th day of the next

Genll. Court, Now if the said THO: MERIWETHER shall appear & prosecute the said appeale & abide the award and Judgmt. of the said Court and pay ye damages of fifteen pr. cent upon ye principall debt damage & costs if cast in the appeal, Then this obligacon to be void otherwise to remain in force

THOMAS MERIWETHER
ROBERT COLEMAN
FRANCIS MERIWETHER

Truely recorded Test FRANCIS MERIWETHER, Cl Cur

pp. 45-46 THIS INDENTURE made the first day of August 1700 Between JAMES MONKESTER of CHARLES COUNTY in ye Provice of MARYLAND, Planter, Eldest Son of JAMES MONKESTER late of the said County & Province deced, Brother of HENRY MONKESTER late of RAPPA. County in ye Colony of Virginia also deced, of the one part and THOMAS MUNDAY of the County of Essex in ye Colony of Virga: aforesd., Planter, of the other part. Witnesseth that for Nineteen pds. Fifteen Shills. lawfull money of England unto ye sd JAMES MONKESTER whereof the said JAMES MONKESTER (party to these pr:sents) doth sell unto the said THOMAS MUNDAY his heires & assignes forever all that tract of land wch: the said HENRY MONKESTER dyed seized of containing Two hundred acres (be ye same more or less) scituate in the abovesd. County of Essex & in ye Parish of Sitting borne on the North side of ye MILL CREEKE it being part of Three hundred acres of land conveyed to ye sd HENRY MONKESTER by JNO. DAINGERFEILD of the said County of RAPPA: by Deed dated ye 5th of May 1671 & acknowledged in ye Court of the sd County of RAPPA: ye 5th: day of July following as may appear by ye Records of ye sd Court And is lawfully come & descended to ye sd JAMES MONKESTER (party to these pr:sents) as heir to ye sd HENRY MONKESTER, his Uncle, with all & singular its rights all houses & buildings all orchards & gardens and all ways profits & hereditaments whatsoever with all rights to the land belonging; To have & to hold ye sd bargained land & every part thereof unto the said THO: MUNDAY his heires & assignes for ever more And the said JAMES MONKESTER (party to these pr:sents) for him selfe his heires doth grant that the said THO: MUNDAY his heires may forever lawfully hold all ye land without the lawfull trouble of ye sd JAMES MONKESTER or any other persons whatsoever (ye yearly rents & services wch: shall grow due in respect to ye premisses aforesd. to our Sovereigne Lord ye King only excepted) In Witness whereof the said parties have set their hands & seales

Signed sealed & delivered in ye pr:sence of

FRANCIS MERIWETHER, JAMES ⊢+⊣ MONKKESTER
JOHN BUTLER
THO: GREGSON

Acknowledged in Essex County Court ye 10th day of 7br: 1700 & truely recorded

Memorand: On ye first day of Augt: 1700 that peaceable possession & seisin ye within menconed lands was delivered by JAMES MONKESTER to THOMAS MUNDAY by Turfe & Twigg to hold to him the said THO: MUNDAY and his heires forever according to the form of ye within written Indenture in ye presence of us

FRANCIS MERIWETHER
JOHN BUTLER
THO: GREGSON

I the within named JAMES MONKESTER do hereby acknowledge to have reced on ye day of ye date of ye Indenture from ye within named THO: MUNDAY ye sum of Nineteen pds. Fifteen shills. being ye consideracon menconed to be paid

Teste FRANCIS MERIWETHER, JAMES ⊢+⊣ MONKESTER
JNO: BUTLER, THO: GREGSON

Acknowledged in Essex County Court ye 10th day of 7br: 1700 & truely recorded

p. 46 KNOW ALL MEN that I JAMES MONKESTER am bound unto THO: MONDAY in ye sum of Thirty nine pds. ten Shills. money of England ye first day of Augt: 1700

The Condicon is that if JAMES MONKESTER truely observe all agreemts. mentioned in Indenture and at the next Court to be held for County of Essex in Virginia to acknowledge ye sd Indenture Then this obligacon to be void otherwise to remain in force

Sealed & delivered in presence of

FRANCIS MERIWETHER, JAMES ⊢+⊣ MONKESTER
JNO: BUTLER
THO: GREGSON

Acknowledged in Essex County Court ye 10th day 7br: 1700 & truely recorded

pp. 46-47 THIS INDENTURE made ye nineth day of Janry: One thousand six hundred ninety & nine Between HARRY BEVERLEY of the County of MIDDLESEX Gent., of the one part and WILLIAM UPSHAW of the County of GLOUCESTER Gent. on the other part

Witnesseth that the sd HARRY BEVERLEY for One hundred pds. Sterl., to him paid doth grant unto the sd WM. UPSHAW his heires and assignes One thousand & seventeen acres of land being in ye County of Essex being part of a devidend of land formerly granted by Patent unto Majr. ROBERT BEVERLEY deced, bounded as followeth, Beginning at a white Oake in Majr. MORRIS's & BUTTONs line being a begining tree of Majr. ROBT. BEVERLEYs whole Patent, thence runing North East to two markt. Maples by the side of GILSONS MAINE RUN so down ye sd RUN to ye point of the Fork where two Runs meet that make ye Fork, thenceup the other Run on to a red Oake markt. with three notches on each side where the Run makes an Elbow close to ye bank, thence West to ye begining before menconed white Oak containing three hundred & three acres, the residue being seven hundred & fourteen acres at the other end of ye before specified Majr. ROBERT BEVERLEYs Patent, begining at a white Oake by a branch near JOHN DOUBTYs House, thence runing South West to a small red Oake markt. with three notches on each side, thence South East to three markt. white Oakes on HOPKINS SWAMP so down the Run to ye sd Swamp to two markt. passimon trees being THOMAS STREACHLEYs corner trees, so along sd STREACHLEYs line North Est. to a Spanish & red Oake the corner of the sd STREACHLEY & JNO. DOUBTYs land by a branch, thence down the sd branch to the begining tree & also all profits & appurtenances belonging unto the said land all rights wch: the said HARRY BEVERLEY his heires & assignes have or may claim To have & to hold unto him the sd WM. UPSHAW his heires & assignes forever, And the said HARRY BEVERLEY for consideracon aforesaid for him & his heires the said hereby granted One thousand & seventy acres of land & premisses will forever warrant & defend And that ye sd WM. UPSHAW his heires & assignes may forever hereafter hold the same without trouble of the said HARRY BEVERLEY his heires or any other persons whatsoever (the quit rents wch: shall hereafter become due to our Sovereign Lord ye King his heires & Successors only Excepted) In Witness whereof wee have set our hand & seales

Signed sealed & delivered in ye pr:sence of us

JOHN SANDERS, HARRY BEVERLEY
THO: S STREACHLY, ELIZABETH BEVERLEY
JOHN I DOUBTY
JAMES RENNOLDS

Acknowledged by HARRY BEVERLEY & ELIZABETH his Wife by FRANCIS MERIWETHER, her Attorney, relinquished her right of Dower thereto in Essex County Court ye 10th day of 7ber: 1700 & truely recorded Test FRANCIS MERIWETHER, Cl Cur

KNOW ALL MEN that I HARRY BEVERLEY do bind myselfe my heirs unto WM.

UPSHAW in ye sum of Two hundred pounds Sterl. witness my hand & seale this 9th day of Janry: 1699

The Condition of this obligacon is that if HARRY BEVERLEY at all times hereafter keep all condicons on his part menconed in Indenture hereof, without fraud or coven, Then this obligacon to be void or else to stand in full force

Signed & delivered in pr:sence of

LEO: TARENT, HARRY BEVERLEY
JOHN ID DOUGHTEE
THOS: 8 STREACHLY

Acknowledged in Essex County Court ye 16th day of 7ber: 1700 & truely recorded

pp. 47-48 THIS INDENTURE made the Nineth day of Janry: One thousand six hundred ninety and nine Between HARRY BEVERLEY of the County of MIDDLESEX Gent. of the one part and JAMES REYNOLDS of County of GLOCESTER on ye other part Witnesseth that the said HARRY BEVERLEY for ye sum of One hundred pounds Sterl. doth sell unto he said JAMES REYNOLDS his heires & assignes one thousand & seventeen acres of land being in Essex County being part of a devidend of land formerly granted by Patent to Majr. ROBERT BEVERLEY deced, bounded as followeth, beining a great white Oake standing by the side of GILSONS MAINE RUN below the Plantacon called BEVERLEYs QUARTER, thence up ye sd Run to a white Oake being a corner tree of THOMAS BLANTONs land, thence South West to a white Oake near a branch that goes up to JNO. DOUBTYs House, thence South West to a small red Oake markt. with three notches on each side, thence North West to a white Oake on a levell, thence North East to an ancient corner white Oake by a small branch, thence East to a red Oake near a branch, thence North to a corner of PELLs land on the South side of a PATH, thence along PELLs line Est., thence North We. to a markt. line that parts this land of REYNOLDS & UPSHAWs land thence East down ye sd line to a red Oake markt. with three notches on each side standing on the bank where ye Run makes an Elbow close to the bank, thence down ye sd Run till it meets with GILSONS MAINE RUN, thence down GILSONS MAINE RUN to ye begining great white Oake, And also all profits & appurtenances belonging unto ye sd One thousand & seventeen acres of land as all rights of wch: ye sd HARRY BEVERLEY his heires hath or may claim by force of ye first originall Patent or Patent deeds or otherwise; To have & to hold unto ye sd JAMES REYNOLDS his heires & assignes for ever And ye sd HARRY BEVERLEY will forever warrant and defend & that ye sd JAMES REYNOLDS his heirs & assignes shall for ever hereafter have the same without trouble of the sd HARRY BEVERLEY his heirs or any other persons wt:soever (the Quit Rents wch: shall hereafter become due only Excepted) In Witness whereof we have set our hands & seale

Signed sealed & delivered in pr:sence of

JOHN SANDERS, HARRY BEVERLEY
THO: 8 STREACHLY ALIZABETH BEVERLEY
JOHN ID DOUBTY
WM. UPSHAW

Acknowledged by HARRY BEVERLEY & ELIZA: his Wife by FRA: MERIWETHER her Attorney relinquished her right of Dower thereto in Essex County Court ye 10th day of 7br: 1700

KNOW ALL MEN that I HARRY BEVERLEY do bind my selfe my heirs unto JAMES REYNOLDS his heires in sum of Two hundred pounds Sterl. Witness my hand & seale this 9th day of Janry: 1699.

The Condition of this obligacon is that if HARRY BEVERLEY at all times hereafter keep all condicons on his part menconed in Indenture hereof without fraud or covin, Then this obligacon to be void or else to stand in full force

Signed & delivered in presence of
LEO: TARENT HARRY BEVERLEY
JOHN I D DOUGHTEE
Acknowledged in Essex County Court ye 10th day of 7ber: 1700 and truely recorded

p. 48 THIS INDENTURE made the Nineth day of Janry: One thousand six hundred ninety & nine Between HARRY BEVERLEY of the County of MIDDLESEX Gent. of the one part & JNO. DOUBTY & THO: GRAVES of the County of Essex, Planters, on ye other part Witnesseth that the sd HARRY BEVERLEY for ye sum of Two thousand and four hundred pounds of tobacco & caske to him in hand truely paid hath sold unto the said JNO. DOUBTY dureing his naturall life & after his decease to the said THO: GRAVES and his heires for ever Two hundred & forty acres of land being in the County of Essex being part of a devident of land formerly granted by Patent to Majr. ROBT. BEVERLEY deced, bounded as followeth, Beginning at a corner white Oake by a great branch & runing thence North Est. to ye land of THOMAS BLANTON deced, wch: he bought of ye sd BEVERLEY, thence along that land South East, thence along a line of markt. trees South West to the land of THO: STREACHLY to a red Oake, thence along the sd STREACHLYs line North West to a Spanish Oake & red Oake by a small branch, thence downe the said small branch to ye main Run of a great branch and thence downe & along the said great branch run to ye begining; And also all profits & appurtenances to ye sd Two hundred & forty acres of land and all the right wch: the sd HARRY BEVERLEY his heirs may claime To have & to hold unto them the sd JNO: DOUGHTY dureing his natural life & after his decease unto THO: GRAVES his heires & assignes for ever And ye said HARRY BEVERLEY ye said land doth grant that ye sd JNO: DOUBTY dureing his natural life & THO: GRAVES & his heires forever shall for ever hereafter hold and injoy the land without interruption of the said HARRY BEVERLEY his heires or any other person (the Quit Rents wch: shall hereafter become due to our Soveraigne Lord ye King only Excepted) In Witness whereof we have set our hands & seales
Signed sealed & delivered in pr:sence of us
WM. UPSHAW, HARRY BEVERLEY
JOHN SANDERS ELIZABETH BEVERLEY
THO: S STREACHLY
JAMES RENNOLDS
Acknowledged by HARRY BEVERLEY & ELIZABETH his Wife by FRA: MERIWETHER her Attorney relinquished her right of Dower thereto in Essex County Court ye 10th day of 7ber: 1700 & truely recorded. Test FRANCIS MERIWETHER, Cl Cur

KNOW ALL MEN by these pr:sents that I ELIZABETH BEVERLEY, Wife of HARRY BEVERLEY of MIDDLESEX County do hereby impower FRANCIS MERIWETHER of the County of Essex to be my true & lawfull Attorney for me to acknowledge & relinquish all my right that I have to One thousand and seventeen acres of land sold by my said Husband to JAMES REYNOLDS, & One thousand & seventeen acres to WM. UPSHAW as aslso Two hundred & forty acres to JNO: DOUBTY & after his deceasse to remaine to his Son in Law THO: GRAVES & his heirs for ever all the said land lying in ye County of Essex between GILSONS MAINE RUN & HOSKINS MAINE RUN & what my said Attorney shall do I do hereby confirm in as full manner as if I were there my selfe personally present In Witness my hand & seale this 3d day of Janry: 1699/1700
Signed & sealed in pr:sence of
WM. JONES, ELIZABETH BEVERLEY
WILL: POTTER
Proved by the Oath of WM. JONES in Essex County Court ye 10th day of 9br: 1700 & truely recorded Test FRANCIS MERIWETHER, Cl Cur

pp. KNOW ALL MEN that wee MARY BILLINGTON, WM. COOPER & HENRY PERKINS of
48- ye County of Essex are firmly bound unto JNO: CATLETT Gent., President of ye sd
49 County Court in sum of Four hundred pds. Sterl. Witness our hands and seales this 10th day of Septembr 1700

The Condition of this obligation is that if ye above bound MARY BILLINGTON, Admrx. of all ye goods & credits of JNO: BILLINGTON deced do make or cause to be made a true and perfect Inventory of all the goods and creditts of ye sd deced wch: have come to ye hands of her the said MARY BILLINGTON And ye same so made do exhibit to ye next Court that shall be held for ye above sd County of Essex and make Oath thereto & ye same well and truely admr. according to Law and further doe make a true and full accot. of her administracon when she shall be thereto lawfully required and all ye rest of ye goods and creditts wch: shall be found ye same being first examined and allowed by ye said Court shall deliver & pay unto such persons respectively as ye sd Court p:rsuant to Law shall appoint, Then this obligation to be void otherwise to remaine in full force
Signed sealed & delivered in ye presence of us

FRANCIS MERIWETHER,
HEN: GOARE

MARY H BILLINGTON
WM. O COOPER
HEN: HP PERKINS

Truely recorded Test FRANCIS MERIWETHER, Cl Cur

p. Virga: Sct. By his Excellency a Proclamacon
49 Whereas his most sacred Majesty by his Royall Letters Pattents bearing date att Westminster the 20th day of July in ye tenth yeare of his Reign was graciously pleased to appoint me FRANCIS NICHOLSON Esqr. to be his Majties. Lieut. & Governor Genll. of this his Majties. Colony & Dominion of Virginia, And whereas his Majesty by his aforesd. Royall Commission to me given, was pleased to declare his Royall will & pleasure that in case of my death or absence from this Colony and Dominion aforesaid and that there be no other person upon the place Commissionated by his Majesty, to be his Majesties Lieutenant Governor or Commander in Cheif that then the present Councill of Virginia do take upon them the Administration of the Government and execute the aforesaid Commission and the severall powers and authorities therein contained and that the first of ye Councill shall preside wth: such power and pre-eminence as any former President hath used & enjoyed, And whereas his Majties. Royall Comands hath been signified to me by ye Rt. Honble. the Lord Commissioners of Trade & Plantations by their Letter dated 12th Aprill 1700 to go to NEW YORK, I have therefore thought fitt to publish and declare, and by this Proclamation in his Majties. name do publish & declare that the Administration of your Government and the Execution of the aforesd. Commission and the severall powers & authorities therein contained is dureing such my absence in his Majesties President and Councill of this his Majesties Colony and Dominion of Virginia And that WILLIAM BYRD Esqr. is at this present the first in the Commission of his Majesties Honable: Councill, And so by reason thereof President, I do therefore hereby in his Majesties named hereby strictly charge require and command all his Majesties loving Subjects of what station or qualification soever within this Colony & Dominion aforesd. to yeild all due honor and obedience to his Majesties aforesd. Royal Commission in the Administration of the Government untill my arrivall here as they will answer the Contrary ( ) of September 1700 in the twelfth yeare of his Majties. reign

A Proclamation declaring Mr. BYRD Esqr. President &c.

FR: NICHOLSON

E. JENNINGS, Depty. Secry.

Published in Essex County Court ye 10th day of 7ber: 1700 and truely recorded

p. 49 Essex Sct. By his Excellency a Proclamation

Whereas I have received an Order from the Rt. Honble: the Lord of the Councill of Trade and Plantations dated att WHITE HALL the 21st day of Febry: 1699 that some time in ye month of November last a Merchants Ship calLed the *JOHN HOPEWELL of LONDON*, where of one HENRY MUNDAY was Comander was plundered by a PIRATE named HENRY KING who formerly used ye PENSYLVANIA TRADE and that some of the said MUNDAYs men voluntaryly forsook him and ran away wth: the said PIRATE upon his Pyraticall Designes, Therefore I FRANCIS NICHOLSON Esqr., his Majties. Lt. and Governr: Generall of Virginia by and with the advice and consent of his Majesties Honble: Councill of State, doe straitly charge and comand all his Majties. Officers Civil and Military and all other his good and loving Subjects whatsoever to use their utmost Endeavour to take seis and apprehend all and every the said PIRATES so as they may be brought to Condign Punishment whose names are HENRY KING, the Grand Pyrate, NICHS. GILLEBRAND, JOHN BURTON, LEONARD RAWLINGS, EDWARD ARTERBERRY, EMANUEL a Portugeze, JOHN SANDERS, WM. PARKER of Sunderland, JOHN HARRIS of London, FRANCIS BROWN a Negroe, being these who deserted the said MUNDAY and I do promise as a reward to any person or persons that shall take seis & aprehend all or any of the sd Pyrate or Pyrates so as such pyrate or pyrates be brought to Justice for the said offences, such person or persons shall have and receive the sume of Twenty pounds Sterl. for every pyrate so taken, and brought to condign punishment, And I likewise straitly charge all Sheriffs to cause this Proclamation to be published in all Churches, Chapellls, Court Houses and other Publick Places in their respective Counties. Given under my hand and his Majesties Seale of the Colony at JAMES TOWN this 9th day of July 1700 in the twelfth yeare of his Majesties Reign

A Proclamation for Aprehending of Pyrates

E. JENNINGS Depty: Secry. FRA: NICHOLSON

Published in Essex County Court ye 10th day of 7ber: 1700 & truely recorded

p. 49 THIS INDENTURE made this forth day of Maye in ye yeare One thousand & seven hundred Betwixt WM. HUDSON & REBECCA his Wife of the County of Essex of ye one pte: & JOHN COPELAND of the aforesaid County of the other pty. Witnesseth that WM. HUDSON & REBECCA his Wife for a valuble consideration of one thousand pounds of sweet scented tobo: & caske to them in hand paid have sold unto the said JOHN COPLAND in aforesaid County now in the tenor of the said WM. HUDSON & REBECCA my Wife the quantity of One hundred acres of land begining upon Mr. HENRY WOODNUTTs line in a branch so runing along the branch side to the DRAGON SWAMP so along the DRAGON SWAMP to a Spanish Oake being a corner tree runing North East to a red Oake standing in Mr. HENRY WOODNUTTs line so runing North North West to a white Oake standing in the head of a Valley & from thence West North West to a Stake & so to the first Station; To have and to hold the said Land unto the said JOHN COPLAN his heirs or assignes for ever with all libertyes & priviledges contained therein and further the same in open Court when legally required with warrante to defend the same from us the sd WM. HUDSON & REBECCA my Wife our heires or assignes for ever whereunto wee have sett our hands and seales

Signed sealed & delivered in the pr:sents of us

HENRY h WOODNOTT, WILLIAM W HUDSON

JNO: SORRELL REBECCA R HUDSON

Acknowledged by WM. HUDSON & REBECCA his Wife by HENRY WOODNOT her Attorney relinquished her right of Dower thereto in Essex County Court the 10th of Septr: 1700 & its truely recorded.

KNOW ALL MEN yt: I REBECCA HUTTSON do apoynt my Father, HENRY WOODNUTT, to be my true lawfull & undoubted Attorney to acknowledge and confirme a tract of land sold by my Husband to JNO. COPLAND of ye same County by a Bill of Saile in Courte redy to be produced, given & by these pr:sents granting unto my said Attorney as full power to act and do for me and in my name as fully as I myselfe might or would do being personally pr:sent there. In Witness hereunto I have set my hand & seale this 9th day of Maye 1700

Sealed and delivered in pr:sents

JNO: SORRELL, REBECKA R HUDSON

HENRY h WOODNUTT

Test FRANCIS MERIWETHER, Cl Cur

p. 50 THIS INDENTURE made ye Eleventh day of July in ye yeare of our Lord God One thousand seven hundred And in the twelfth yeare of ye Reign of our Sovereign Lord Wm., King over England &c., Between JOHN BAKER of KINGSTONE Pish. in ye County of GLOUCESTER of ye one pte: and WILLIAM BASTYN of ye aforesd. Pish & County of ye other pte: Witnesseth yt: ye sd JNO. BAKER for the sume of Fifty pounds of good sweet scented tobacco to him payd doth sell unto the sd WILLIAM BASTYN his Exers. & assignes one hundred & eighteen acres of land be it more or less being part of a tract of land commonly called by ye name of BUTTONS RANG containing Three thousand six hundred & fifty acres being in ye Pish. of Sittenburne in ye County of Essex & granted formerly to Mr. THOMAS BUTTON deced by Patent dated ye 19th day of July 1666, wch: sd tract was given by ye last Will and Testament of ye sd THOMAS BUTTON to his Brother, ROBERT BUTTON, as by ye sd Will dated ye first day of March 1669 will more plainly appeare & since by ye heires of ye sd ROBT. BUTTON conveyed to the abovesd. JNO. BAKER as by an Order of ye President of Councill to him granted at JAMES CITTY & dated ye 27th day of October 1688 may & will appeare, which sd p:cell of land reputed to be One hundred & eighteene acres is bounded as followeth; Berginning at a corner tree of MATTRUM WRIGHTs line towards ye North West side of ASSAGES BRANCH running a long ye sd MATTRUM WRIGHTs & WM. WILLIAMS line to ANTHONY SAMUELLs line & along ANTHONY SAMUELLs & BARBERs line to ye line of ye grand Pattent & a long ye sd line to ye first specified place, Together withall woods housing fencing orchards & appurtenances to ye sd land belonging unto ye sd WM. BASTYN his Exers. & assignes from ye day next before ye date hereof unto ye sd WM. BASTYN during ye tearme of one year from thence next ensueing to ye intent that by vertue thereof, & ye Statute for ye transferrying of uses into possession ye sd WM. BASTYN may be in actual possession of ye sd land & be enabled to accept a grant & release of ye premisses. In Wittness whereof ye sd JOHN BAKER sett his hand & seale

Signed sealed & delivered in presence of us

GEORGE AXE, JOHN BAKER

THOMAS FLEPPIN

WILLM. ARMISTEAD

Acknowledged in Essex County Court ye 10th day of 7ber 1700 and truely recorded

pp. 50-51 THIS INDENTURE made ye twelfth day of July in ye yeare of our Lord God One thousand seven hundred Betweene JOHN BAKER of KINGSTONE Pish: in ye County of GLOCESTER of ye one pte: and WILLIAM BASTYN of ye aforesd. Pish: & County of ye other part Witnesseth that for ye sum of Three thousand five hundred pounds of good sweet scented tobacco & cask by ye sd WM. BASTYN in hand payd ye sd JNO: BAKER hath granted unto ye sd WM. BASTYN his heirs & assignes forever in ye actuall possession of ye sd WM. BASTYN now being by vertue of an Indenture of Lease to him made bearing date the day next before ye date of these presents and of ye Statute for transferring uses into possession, One hundred & Eighteene acres of land, And it shall be lawfull for ye sd WM. BASTYN his heires & assignes at all tymes forever hereafter peaceably & quietly to hold ye sd p:cell of land without ye lawfull lett of him ~~ye sd~~ JNO: BAKER his heires or assignes or any other p:sons claiming under him (ye Quit Rents from henceforth to grow due for ye pr:misses only excepted & foreprized) And ye sd JNO: BAKER will personally appeare by himselfe or his lawfull Attorney before ye Justices of ye sd Court & will acknowledge this Instrument of Writing unto ye sd WM. BASTYN his heires & assignes and alsoe ye sd JNO: BAKER doth hereby bind himselfe his heires that ELIZABETH his Wife shall likewise within Six months after her arrivall into Virginia appear before ye abovesd Court & accordingly relinquish her right of Dower to ye above pr:misses In Witness whereof ye sd JOHN BAKER hereto sett his hand & Seale

Signed sealed & delivered in ye presence of us
GEORGE AXE, JOHN BAKER
THOMAS FLEPPIN
WILLM. ARMISTEAD

Acknowledged in Essex County Court ye 10th day of 7ber: 1700 & truly recorded

KNOW ALL MEN yt. I JOHN BAKER am firmly bound unto WILLIAM BASTYN in ye full sume of Seaven thousand pounds of good sweet scented tobacco & caske to containe ye same dated ye twelfth day of July in ye yeare of our Lord God One thousand seven hundred

The Conditionm of this pr:sent obligation is that whereas JOHN BAKER hath by his Deed of Lease dated ye Eleventh day of this Instant moneth July sold unto WM. BASTYN one hundred & eighteen acres of land and by his Deed of Release dated with these pr:sents for ye valuable consideration confirmed to ye sd WM. BASTYN his heires & assignes ye sd p:cell of land reputed to be One hundred and Eighteene acres If therefore ye above named WILLIAM BASTYN shall at all tymes forever from henceforth peaceably hold ye sd p:cell of land clearly dischrged from all manner of suits incumbrances done by ye above bounden JOHN BAKER and also if ye sd JNO. BAKER shall hereafter at the reasonable request & at ye cost & charges of ye sd WM. BASTYN generally doe & execute all other act & thing needfull for ye full confirming ye tytle & estate of ye above p:cell of land Then this present obligation to be voyd or else to stand in full force

Signed sealed & delivered in ye presence of us
GEORGE AXE, JOHN BAKER
THOMAS FLEPPIN
WILLM. ARMISTEAD

Acknowledged in Essex County Court ye 10th day of 7ber: 1700 and truely recorded

pp. KNOW ALL MEN by these pr:sents that I HESTER, and now Wife of ANDREW DUD-
51- DIN, of ye County of Essex, doe with the advice & consent of my saide Husband
52 and for divers good causes & especially for a valluable consideration already
reced. have sold and made over unto Mr. DANLL. DOBYNS of the County aforesd. all my right & interest of Two hundred acres of land wch: I formerly bought of JOHN DICK as by an Assignment on ye back side of a Deed of Sale made over unto JOHN DICK his Father, & confirmed by JOHN & GEORGE KILLMAN, yn: of RAPPAH: County, the said land scituate in ye County of Essex according to Survey of the same made by GEORGE MORRIS wch: said Two hundred acres of land boundeth as followeth; beginning at a Spanish Oake in the line of Capt. JOSIAS PICKES nigh GREEN BRANCH & runing thence

over GREENE BRANCH So:W: to a red Oake on a level, thence No:W: to a red Oake by a small branch, thence over certain small branches belonging to the GREEN BRANCH aforesd. parralell unto ye first line to ye land of Capt. JOSIAS PICKES as aforesd. to a white Oake corner, thence to the first mentioned station; To have & to hold the foresd. land to him ye sd Mr. DANLL. DOBYN his heires & assignes forever withall ye priviledges wth: woods & waters in as large ample manner as it is assigned to me the sd HESTER DUDDIN, then HESTER DICK & further the sd HESTER DUDDIN doe oblige my selfe my heires to save harmless the sd DANLL. DOBYNS his heires & assignes agt: any persons that shall molest the said DANIEL DOBYNS his heires or assignes claimeing any tytle and to acknowledge this my act and deed in ye County so soon as required. In Testimony of the same, I have hereunto put my hand & seale this 20th day of August 1700
Signed sealed & delivered in the pr:sence of

ARON S PERRY,   HESTER ED DUDDIN
HENRY B PRESCOTT

HEN: WOODNUTT by vertue of a Power of Attorney from HESTER DUDDIN acknowledged this Deed in Essex County Court ye 10th day of 7ber: 1700 and truely recorded

KNOW ALL MEN by these presents that I HESTER, the Wife of ANDREW DUDDIN, of the County of Essex being through age & Indisparition of body uncapable of going to Court, doe constitute & ordaine my good & trusty friend, HENRY WOODNUTT, for me & in my stead to be my true & lawfull Attorney to acknowledge for me & in my behalfe a Deed of Sale wch: I by & wth: the consent of my sd Husband, ANDREW DUDDIN, have made over unto DANLL. DOBYNS as firmly and amply as if I my selfe were there present In Witness hereunto I have sett my hand and seale this 9th day of Sept: 1700
Signed sealed & delivered in ye presence of us

ARON S PERRY   HESTER ED DUDDIN
HENRY B PRESCOTT

Truely recorded p FRANCIS MERIWETHER Cl Cur

P. IN THE NAME OF GOD Amen. I ROBERT TAYLOR of South farnham Parrish in ye
52 County of Essex being very sick and weak, but of perfect sence & memory thanks be to God, doe now think fitt to make my last Will and Testament in manner and form following, first, I recommend my selfe into the hands of my Creator trusting and assuredly believing in ye free pardon and forgiveness of all my sins in & through the merits and mediation of my Lord and Saviour Jesus Christ and my body to be desently entered in the Earth at the descretion of my Executors here after named, And as for that worldly Estate it hath pleased God to bestow upon me I dispose of as followeth

I will that my funerall and other charges and all kind of debts that shall apear justly due to any persons whatsoever from me be duely and truely satisfied out of my Estate by my Executrix here after named

Item I give and bequeath unto my loveing Wife, HANAH TAYLOR, all my reall and personall moveable and unmoveable, being in what nature soever with the plantation and two hundred acres of land there unto belonging, dureing her naturall life And after her dissease it shall go to BENJAMIN COOK and to his heirs & assigns forever

Item I give & bequeath to THOMAS HUCHISON, the Son of CHARLES HUCHISON, one hundred acres of land out of the land I now live on to have in his possession as soon as he shall come to be of age; but if he should dy before he should come to ye age, then it shall fall to the aforesaid BENJAMIN COOK and to his heirs & assignes forever

Lastly I doe hereby ordaine & constitute my now loving Wife, HANAH TAYLOR, to be my whole Executrix of this my last Will and Testament revoking & making void all other

Will or Wills heretofore made. In Witness whereof I have hereunto sett my hand and afixed my seal this 7th day of September 1699

Test JAMES WOOD, ROBERT RT TAYLOR
ROBERT LEWIS

Proved by ye Oaths of ye witnesses in Essex County Court ye 10th day of 7br: 1700 and truely recorded Test FRANCIS MERIWETHER, Cl Cur

p. 52 KNOW ALL MEN by these pr:sents that I ANDREW SIMPSON of LONDON, Mercht., have named & constituted my trusty friend, ROBT: COLEMAN (of Essex County in Virginia) my true & lawfull Attorney for me to demand & receive all sums of money or tobaccos yt: is in any way due to me or to any person who I am imployed by or for, granting to my said Atturney my full power & lawfull authority to use & execute all such things & devisses in ye Law as shall be thought fitt by my said Atturney for ye recovering of all or any part of ye Debts aforesaid, & acquittances or other discharges to make in my name & generally to doe & receive in ye premisses as fully as I my selfe might doe being personally present, confirming wt: my said Atturney shall act & lawfully doe therein In Witness whereof I have sett my hand & fixed my seale this fourth day of May 1700

Signed sealed & delivered in ye presence of
LEONARD CHAMBERLAINE ANDREW SIMPSON
JAMES REEVES
WILLIAM JORDAN

Prov'd by ye oathes of LEONARD CHAMBERLAINE & JAMES REEVES in Essex County Curt ye 10th day of 7ber: 1700 & truely recorded. Test FRANCIS MERIWETHER, Cl Cur

p. 52 KNOW ALL MEN by these presents that I NICHOLAS FRENCH of LEVERPOOL in the County of LANCASTER, Mariner, have named my trusty frind, ROBERT COLEMAN, of Essex County in Virginia my true & lawfull Atturney for me to demand sue for recover & receive all such sums of money or tobacco that is in any wise due to me or to any person whom I am Imployed by, or that is in any way due to me granting to mys d Atturney my full power to use & execute all such things in the Law as shall be thought fit by my sd Atturney for the recoverying of all or any part of the debts aforesaid and acquittances or other discharges to make & give in my name and generally to do as fully as I myselfe might or could doe, being personally present, allowing all & whatsoever my sd Atturney shall act or lawfully doe therein In Witness where of I have set my hand & fixed my seale this (blank) 1700

Signed sealed & delivered in ye presence of us
LEONARD CHAMBERLAINE, NICHOLAS FRENCH
JAMES REEVES

Proved by ye oathes of ye Witnesses thereto in Essex County Court ye 10th day of 7ber: 1700 & truely recorded Test FRANCIS MERIWETHER, Cl Cur

p. 52 KNOW ALL MEN by these presents that we JNO: WATERS, WM. YOUNG & RICHD. JONES of ye County of Essex are bound unto JNO: CATLETT, Gent. President of ye sd County Court in ye sum of Fifty pds. Sterl. wee bind ourselves Witness our hands & seales this 10th day of 7ber: 1700

The Condition of this obligation is that if ye above bound JOHN WATERS, Guardian of ELIZA: COLELOUGH his heirs & Admrs. shall truely pay unto he sd ELIZ: COLELOUGH all such Estate as now is or hereafter shall come to ye hands of ye sd JNO. WATERS as soon as ye sd ELIZ: COLELOUGH shall attaine to lawfull age or when thereunto required by ye

Justices of ye peace for Essex County Court also to save ye sd Justices their heirs from damages that may arise about ye sd Estate, Then the above obligation to be void otherwise to remaine in full power
Signed sealed & delivered in pr:sence of us
FRANCIS MERIWETHER, JOHN WATERS
THOS: HUCKLESCOTT WILLM. YOUNG
RICHARD JONES
Truely recorded Test FRANCIS MERIWETHER, Cl Cur

p. 53 KNOW ALL MEN that wee MARY COVINGTON, JAMES BOUGHAN & JNO: BROOKS of ye County of Essex are firmly bound unto JNO: CATLETT Gent. President of ye sd County Court in ye sum of Six hundred pounds Sterl. to true payment wee bind ourselves our heirs Witness our hands and seales this 10th day of September 1700
The Condition of this obligation is yt: if ye above bound MARY COVINGTON, Admx. of all and singular ye goods chattles and creditts of THO: COVINGTON deced, do make a true and perfect Inventory of all ye goods chattles and creditts wch: shall come to ye hands of her and ye same to exhibitt to ye next Court that shall be held for ye abovesd. County of Essex and make oath to ye same, And further doe make a true & just account of her Administration when she shall be thereunto lawfully required and upon ye same being first examined and allowed of by ye sd Court shall deliver & pay unto such persons as ye Court shall appoint, Then this obligation to be void otherwise to remain in full force
Signed sealed and delivered in ye pr:sence of us
SALVATOR MUSCOE, MARY X COVINGTON
THOMAS HUCKLESCOTT JAMES BOUGHAN
JOHN BROOKS
Truely recorded Test FRANCIS MERIWETHER, Cl Cur

p. 53 IN THE NAME OF GOD Amen, I JOHN SORRELL of Essex County being sicke & weake in body but of sound & perfect memory praised be God for ye same, doe make & ordaine this my last Will & Testament in manner & forme following, First I give & bequeath my soule to God that gave it in hopes of a glorious resurrection att ye last day & my body to ye Earth to be decently intered after my decease & for my temporall Estate I give & dispose of in manner & forme following; my will & designe is that after my just debts are satisfyed & payd, I give & bequeath to my Wife, DORCAS SORRELL, One thousand pounds of Tobo: & for ye remaindr: of my Estate my desire is yt: itt shalbe equally divided amongst my Children, vizt., JAMES, JNO., EVE SORRELL & ye Child wch: my (wife) is with Child withall, Lastly I ordaine my loveing Wife, DORCAS SORRELL, sole Executrix of this my last Will and Testament In Testimony whereof I have hereunto set my hand and seale this thirty day of Aprill 1700
Signed sealed & delivered in presence of
ROBT. BROOKE, JOHN SORELL
GEORGE ┗ DOBBINS
Prov'd by ye Oath of Mr. ROBT. BROOKE in Essex County Court ye 10th day of 7ber: 1700 and truely recorded

KNOW ALL MEN by these presents that wee DORCAS SORRELL, RAND: BIRD & RICHD. GOOGY of the County of Essex are firmly bound unto JNO: CATLETT Gent., President of the sd County Court in ye sume of Twenty thousand pounds of good tobo: to the true payment whereof we bind ourselves Witness our hands & seales this 11th day of Septr: 1700
The Condition of this obligation is such that if ye above bound DORCAS SORRELL who at

a Court held for Essex County the 10th day of this Instant obtained a Probate of the last Will and Testament of JNO: SORRELL deceased, shall at all times hereafter perform & fullfill the sd Will fully pay and satisfie all such Legatees as there in are expressed and perform all the Law enjoyns in such cases, Then ye above obligation to be void, otherwise to remain in force

Signed sealed & delivered in the presence of us

THOMAS HUCKLESCOTT, FRANCIS MERIWETHER

DORCAS X SORRELL
RANDOLPH O BIRD
RICHARD 4 GOOGIE

Truely recorded Test FRANCIS MERIWETHER, Cl Cur

pp. 53-54 IN THE NAME OF GOD, Amen. I JOHN PEATLE of ye Parish of Sittingbourne & County of Essex being sick & weak of body but of sound & perfect mind & memory praise be there fore given to Almighty God, do make & ordaine this my last Will & Testament in maner & forme following, (this is to say) First & principally I comend my soul into the hands of Almighty God hopeing through ye Meritts death & passion of my Saviour Jesus Christ to have full & free pardon & forgiveness of all my sins, also inherit everlasting life, & my body I comit to ye earth to be decently to be decently buried at ye discretion of my Executrix here after named, And as touching ye disposition of all such temporall Estate as it hath pleased Almighty God to bestow upon me I give & dispose thereof as followeth:

First I will that all my debts & funerall charges shall be paid & discharged

Item I give unto THO: MUNDAY, ye Son of THOMAS MUNDAY, my largest Stilliards with Pee & Canhooks belonging to them

Item I give unto JOHN MUNDAY, ye Son of THOMAS MUNDAY, my other Stilliards with Pee & Canhooks belonging to them

Item I give unto SARAH MUNDAY, ye Wife of THOMAS MUNDAY, a hogshead of tobacco of mine lying att ye house of FRANCIS JAMES in RICHMOND County under my own marke

Item I give & bequeath unto FRANCES MUNDAY & MARTHA MUNDAY, ye Daughters of THO: MUNDAY equally between them a hogshead of tobacco of me at Mr. THO: PEIRCEs in RICHMOND County under my own marke

Item I give unto HANAH MUNDAY, Daughter of THOMAS MUNDAY, my Trunck with lock & key

Item I give unto CHARLES MUNDAY, ye Son of THOMAS MUNDAY, my two yards & three quarters of braod cloth now in ye house of ye sd THOMAS MUNDAY

Item I give unto JOSEPH MUNDAY, ye Son of THOMAS MUNDAY, my remnant of speckled dimity, also now in ye sd THOMAS MUNDAYs house

Item I give unto THOMAS MUNDAY my best Carolina Hatt

Item I give unto THO: MUNDAY & JOHN MUNDAY, Sons of THO: MUNDAY, each of them two pair of shoes that are in my Chest & all my Bookes equally between them

Item All the rest & residue of my Estate, goods & chattles whatsoever, I do give & bequeath unto HANAH MUNDAY who I make full & sole Executrix of this my last Will & Testament and I do hereby revoke & make void all former Wills & Testaments by me heretofore made. In Witness whereof I ye sd JOHN PEATLE to this my last Will & Testament have sett my hand & seale ye day & year aforesaid

Signed Sealed & declared by JNO: PEATLE to be his last Will & Testament in presence of

THO: WINSLOW, JOHN PARKER

Ye marke of
JOHN IP PEATLE

Prov'd by ye oathes of THOMAS WINSLOW & JNO: PARKER Witnesses thereto in Essex County Court ye 11h day of 7br: 1700 & adm. with ye Will annexed granted to THOMAS MUNDAY on ye sd deceds Estate dureing ye Minority of HANAH MUNDAY, his Daughter, Exex. herein named, And truely recorded Test FRANCIS MERIWETHER Cl Cur

KNOW ALL MEN by these pr:sents that wee THO: MUNDAY, THO: GREGSON & THOMAS HUCKLESCOTT of ye County of Essex are firmly bound unto JNO. CATLETT Gent. President of ye County Court in ye Sum of Fifty pds. Sterl. to ye true payment we bind ourselves Witness our hands and seales this 11th day of 7br: 1700

The Condition of this obligation is yt: if ye above bound THO: MUNDAY, Admr. to ye Will annexed of JNO: PEATLE deced, dureing ye minority of HANNAH MUNDAY, his Daughter, Exex. therein named, do make a true & perfect Inventory of all ye goods chattells and creditts of ye sd deced & do exhibit to ye next Court that shall be held for ye abovesd County and do well & truely administer according to Law and further make or cause to be made a true & just account of his administration and shall deliver & pay unto such p:sons as ye sd Court p:sunat to Law shall appoint, Then this obligation to be void otherwise to remaine in ful force

Signed sealed & delivered in ye presence of us

HEN: GOARE	THO: TM MUNDAY
FRANCIS MERIWETHER	THO: GREGSON
	THO: HUCKLESCOTT

Truely recorded Test FRANCIS MERIWETHER, Cl Cur

p. 54 IN OBEDIENCE to Order of the Worshipfull Court of Essex bearing date ye 11th day of July 1700 wee whose names are subscribed & seales affixed being summoned as Jurors & sworne before Mr. SAML. THACKER to goe upon ye Land of JNO: PARKER together wth: Mr. CHARLES SMITH, Surveyor, upon ye 25th of July 1700 & to lay out the same & value ye damage if any comitted by BENJAMIN STONE, Defendt., did upon the said day together with the said CHARLES SMITH goe upon ye sd land and lay out the same & do find ye Defendt. trespasser & ye damage Ten Shillings

EMUND PAGETT,	WM. DYER his marke D	JNO. GRAVES
JNO. DAINGERFEILD	JOHN BUTCHER	THO: ⊣ DAVIS
THO: TM MUNDAY	ROBT. CP MILLS	WM. M JONES
RICHD. STOKES	WM. AYRES	WALTER + JONES

Truely recorded Test FRANCIS MERIWETHER, Cl Cur

p. 54 Upon the back of an Attachmt. granted to FRANCIS SMITH agt: ye Estate of JNO. SMITH for L 14...4...6 was made ye following return

Essex sc. Augt. ye 5th 1700. Attached one red Cow & Calfe, one black Steer, two ruggs, a pair of blanketts, two pewter dishes, two pewter candlesticks, a pewter tankard, & a pewter porringer, a red steer & young red Cow

p THOMAS HUCKLESCOTT Sub Sher:

pp. 54-55 THIS INDENTURE made the Eleventh day of September 1700 Betweene THOMAS MUNDAY of the Parish of Sittingburne & County of Essex, Planter, of ye one part & THOMAS WINSLOW of the same Parish & County, Tayler, of the other part.

Wittnesseth that for the sum of Seven pds. Ten shillings good & lawfull money of England ye sd THO: MUNDAY hath granted unto ye sd THOMAS WINSLOW his heirs & assignes all that tract of land containing One hundred acres (be the same more or less) scituate & being in the aforesd. Parish & County And is part of a devident of Two hundred acres of land purchased by the sd THOMAS MUNDAY of JAMES MONKESTER of

CHARLES COUNTY of the Province of MARYLAND by Deed bearing date ye first day of Augt. last past to wit that part of the said Two hundred acres wch: lyeth on ye lower side of a Swamp called by the name of (? CORSTONS) DEEP and ye run of ye sd Swamp to be the bounds between the said THOMAS MUNDAY & THOMAS WINSLOW with all its rights & houses & buildings whatsoever thereupon standing and all orchards gardens woods and all wayes waters profits & hereditaments and every part thereof & all ye estate right, To have and to hold unto ye sd THO: WINSLOW his heirs & assignes for ever And the sd THO: MUNDAY for himselfe his heirs doth grant in manner following (vizt.) that the said THO: WINSLOW his heirs shall forever lawfully occupy & enjoy all the land wtih the appurtenances without interruption of the sd THO: MUNDAY his heirs or assignes or any persons claiming under him And that sd THO: MUNDAY shall at the reasonable request & at ye costs & charges in ye Law of ye sd THO: WINSLOW his heirs or assignes do acknowledge further conveyances in ye Law for absolute conveying of ye aforemenconed land as shall be required In Witness whereof ye sd parties have set their hands & seales

Signed sealed & delivered in presence of us
FRA: TALIAFERRO, THOMAS M MUNDAY
LEO: HILL 1700
ROBT. MOBLEY

Acknowledged by THO: MUNDAY & right of Dower relinquished by SARAH, his Wife, in Essex County Court ye 11th day of 7ber: 1700 & truely recorded

p. Sr. I desire ye may appear as Attorney for me & Compa: in all causes whereon
55 we are concerned in Essex Court & ye will oblige Sr. yor: humble Servt.
Aprill 11th 1700
To Capt. THO: GREGSON these JA: CHRISTIE
Truely recorded Test FRANCIS MERIWETHER, Cl Cur

p. Upon ye back of an Attachmt. granted to Mr. BENJA: MOSELEY agt: ye Estate of
55 JNO: SMITH JUNR., for 1460 pds. of tobo: & twenty five Shills, Sterl. money was made ye following return:
Essex Sc. Aug: ye 2d 1700. Attacht. one feather bed & bolster & a pair of sheets & a white gelding branded TI
p THOMAS HUCKLESCOTT, Sub Sher:
Truely recorded Test FRANCIS MERIWETHER, Cl Cur

pp. THIS INDENTURE made the ninth day of October 1700 Between RICHARD LEIGH-
55- TON of the Parish of Sittingburne in ye County of Essex within ye Colony of Vir-
56 ginia, Planter, of ye one part and THO: GREGSON of ye same Parish County & Colony of the other part. Witnesseth that for Five thousand pounds of good sound merchantable Tobo: unto ye sd RICHD. LEIGHTON in hand already paid sold unto ye sd THOMAS GREGSON his heirs & assignes forever all that tract of land containing Four hudnred seventy & eight acres being in the Parish of Sitting burne & County of Essex aforesd. bounded as follows Beginning at a red Oake corner tree to JNO: SPIERS standing by the old road side, thence North East to a red Oake corner tree of Mr. WILLIAMS, thence through a great Pocoson to another red Oake corner tree to WILLIAMS, thence South East to a white Oake corner tree to COOK & INGRAM, thence along the sd INGRAMs line South South West to a Hickory standing in the line of EDWARD MOSELEY, thence along ye sd MOSELEYs line North to a white Oake standing in ye edge of a Pocoson, thence West by & near the said Pocoson to a live Oake standing in ye Pocoson the

which parts this land & the land of the sd SPIERS, thence North to ye place it began, together with all houses & structures orchards gardens trees & appurtenances wt:soever belonging & all ye estate right of him the said RICHD. LEIGHTON in the same wch: sd Devident is part of a Devident of Six hundred thirty & eight acres of land granted to ye sd RICHD. LEIGHTON by Patent bearing date ye 23d day of Aprill 1688; To have & to hold unto him the said THO: GREGSON forever more he ye sd THO: GREGSON paying ye rents & p:forming ye services wch: shall hereafter become due unto our Sovereigne Lord ye King And the sd RICHD. LEIGHTON for himselfe & his heirs ye sd land will warrant & for ever defend and doth promise ye sd THO: GREGSON his heirs & assignes shall at all times for ever hereafter lawfully enter into possess & enjoy ye sd land without denial of ye sd RICHARD LEIGHTON his heirs or any other persons In Witness whereof ye parties their hands & seales have set

Signed sealed & delivered in ye presence of us

FRANCIS GOULDMAN, RICHARD LEIGHTON
SAML. THACKER
FRANCIS MERIWETHER

Acknowledged by RICHARD LEIGHTON & right of Dower relinquished by JUDITH his Wife in Essex County Court ye 10th day of October 1700 and truely recorded

KNOW ALL MEN by these presents that I RICHD. LEIGHTON am bound unto THO: GREGSON of ye same County in ye sum of Ten thousand pounds of good merchantable tobo: & caske dated ye 9th day of October 1700

The Condition of this obligacon is that if RICHD. LEIGHTON his heirs shall keep all ye Covenants yt: are or ought to be observed in one pair of Indentures between ye sd RICHD. LEIGHTON and THOMAS GREGSON of ye other part Then this obligacon to be void or else to remain in full force

Signed sealed & delivered in presence of us

FRANCIS GOULDMAN RICHD. LEIGHTON
SAML. THACKER
FRANCIS MERIWETHER

Acknowledged in Essex County Court ye 10th day of October 1700 & truely recorded

p. Virga: At JAMES CITY 10th July 1700
56 In the 12th year of the Reign of King Wm. ye Third over England &c.

Present his Excellency in Councill

Ordered that if any Writts issue for a New Election of any Burgesses in ye stead of any who being members of the House are either removed by death or departed out of the Country, that in every such case yt: ye Sher: of the respective Counties to who such Writts issue shall be directed to take especiall care that there be no undue Elections made but that the same be done according to ye severall Lawes in that case made & provided And ye Courts of each respective County & Counties within this his Majties. Colony & Dominion of Virga: are hereby directed & required to take especiall care that ye aggreivances (of their respective Inhabitants) if any such there be, be duly & legally certified according to Law

DIONISIUS WRIGHT

Published in Essex County Court ye 10th day of October 1700 & truely recorded

pp. Virga; ss. By his Excellency
56- In pursuance to an Act of Assembly made at JAMES CITY ye 8th day of June in
57 ye 32d year of ye Reign of our Sovereign Lord Charles ye Second of ever blessed memory and in ye year of our Lord 1680 & by ye authority thereof & ye

power therein granted, I FRA: LORD HOWARD, Baron of EFFINGHAM, his Majties Lt. & Govr: Genll. of Virga: do by this Publick Instrumt. under my hand & ye Seale of the Colony of Virga: pronounce Publish & deliver CORNELIUS NOELL, borne in HOLLAND, professing ye Protestant Religion & first haveing taken ye Oathes of Allegiance & paid ye fees therein menconed according to ye Tenor of ye sd Act to be fully & compleatly Naturalized and I do hereby fully & compleatly Naturalize him ye sd CORNELIUS NOELL giveing & granting unto him & his heirs forever all & singular ye priviledges and immunities & rights of ye Inhabitants of this Colony of Virga: And that as fully & amply to all intents & purposes wt:soever as if he ye sd CORNELS: NOELL had been borne within this his Majties. Dominion as any other his Majties. naturall borne Subjects wt:soever have or ought or do in any part enjoy any former Law usage or custom to ye contrary notwithstanding. Given under my hand & ye seale of ye Colony this 27th day of Aprill 1686

Truely recorded according to an Ordr. of Essex County Court ye 19th day of 8br: 1700
Test FRANCIS MERIWETHER, Cl Cur

EFFINGHAM

p. 57 THIS INDENTURE made this 10th day of October in ye year of our Lord God 1700 and in ye 12th year of the Reign of our Sovereign Lord William by the grace of God of England &c. Betweene JNO: GAINES of Farnham Pish. in the County of Essex, Planter, of ye one part and PETER TREBLE of the same place, Cooper, of the other part, Witnesseth that the said JNO. GAINES for a certaine parcell of land lying upon HOSKINS CREEKE transferred over unto him by the sd PETER TREBLE at or before ye ensealing & by & with ye free & voluntary consent of SARAH my now lawfull Wife have granted exchanged sold unto he sd PETER TREBLE his heirs & assigns forever a certain peice of land being in ye aforesd. County of Essex containing One hundred & Fifty acres more or less, being part of a Thousand acres of land granted by Patent to Mr. THO: GAINES of the Pish: and County aforesd., ye sd Thousand acres lying on ye Maine Pocoson of PISCATTAWAY CREEKE nxt above ye land of RICHD. HOLT ye boundes of ye sd land beginning at a marked white Oake standing by a branch side between ANN BURNETTs & JOHN GAINES & soe running up a gully to a marked Gum & from thence to a marked Hickory by he PATH side that leades from ye WIDOW BURNETTs to ye sd ANN BURNETTs & so along ye sd PATH untill it meets with ye line of JNO. BURNETT that divides ye sd JNO. BURNETT & JOHN GAINES land at a marked red Oake & along ye sd line into ye maine Swamp of PISCATTAWAY CREEK & along ye maine Swamp to ye aforesd. ANN BURNETTs Branch and up the sd Branch to ye first begining as by ye afore recited Patent will more at large appear; To have & to hold ye sd parcell of land unto ye sd PETER TREBLE & unto his heirs & assigns forever together with all houses fencings orchards grounds thereunto belonging to ye use of ye sd PETER TREBLE & his heirs & assigns forever, he paying unto our Sovereign ye King all such Rents & Duties as may hereafter become due for ye sd premises hereby transferred and I ye sd JNO. GAINES together with SARAH my Wife do grant that we will acknowledge this Instrument of Writeing as our act & deed to ye use of the sd PETER TREBLE to the purport thereof in any Court that shall be held for the abovesd. County of Essex when required for his or their peaceable possession of the premisses In Witness whereof we have hereunto set our hands & fixed our seales

Signed sealed & delivered in ye presence of us
LEONARD CHAMBERLINE
ARGOLE BLACKSTAN
JA: CLERKE

JOHN GAINES
SARAH S GAINES

KNOW ALL MEN by these presents that I SARAH GAINES do hereby appoint my loveing friend, Mr. LEO: CHAMBERLAINE, my lawfull Attorney to acknowledge my right of Dower of this within menconed Deed of Sale from me or my assignes as Witness my hand this 10th day of October 1700
Signed sealed & delivered in presence of
ARGOL BLACKSTON SARAH GAINES
JA: CLERKE
The within Deed was acknowledged by JNO: GAINES and SARAH his Wife her right of Dower relinquished by LEO: CHAMBERLAINE according to ye above Power in Essex County Court ye 10th day of October 1700 & is truely recorded as also ye sd Power

pp. THIS INDENTURE made ye Sixth day of December One thousand six hundred
57- ninety & seven Between THOMAS PETTIS of KING & QUEEN County in Virga: of
58 ye one part and PETER TREBLE of the said County on ye other part Witnesseth
that I ye sd THO: PETTIS for the full quantity of Two hundred sixty four acres of land transferred over unto me & my heirs &c. by the sd PETER TREBLE by way of Exchange at ye ensealing & delivery hereof have granted unto ye sd PETER TREBLE & to his heirs & assignes for ever all that parcell of land that I hold by Patent bearing date ye 20th day of October 1691 & granted unto me the said THOMAS PETTIS under ye broad Seale of this Colony containing Ninety three acres of land being in South Farnham Parish in ye County of Essex formerly called & known by the name of RAPPAHANNOCK County in Virga: aforesd., when the sd Patent was granted ye sd land being bounded as followeth, begining at two corner red Oakes standing by the mouth of HOSKINS CREEK corner of a parcell of land granted unto Mr. ROBT. YARD & Mr. JOHN WATERS and runing thence by their lands South East to a corner tree in the WHITE OAKE SWAMP, thence South West to a Stake between two Oak saplins, thence North West by North to three Spanish Oak saplins in the Stake at the head of a Marsh or Gutt and thence down & alongst ye Marsh including all points of high land to the place it began; To have & to hold ye aforesd. Ninety three acres of land and all its rights & appurtenances together with the houses fences orchards and all the conveniences to the same belonging unto him the sd PETER TREBELL & to his heirs & assignes for ever, they paying unto our Sovereign Lord ye King all such quit rents as shall become due for ye sd land And I ye sd THO: PETTIS do further oblige me my heirs that he at all times forever hereafter have & enjoy the hereby premisses without interruption of me them or my heirs In Witness whereof I have hereunto set my hand & afixed my seale
Signed sealed & delivered in ye presence of us
PHIL: PENDLETON, THO: PETTIS
ED: EASTHAM
GEORGE EASTHAM
Acknowledged & right of Dower relinquished in Essex County Court ye 10th day of March 1698 & truely recorded Test FRANCIS MERIWETHER, Cl Cur

KNOW ALL MEN by these pr:sents that I PETER TREBLE of Essex County, Cooper, together with ELIZA: TREBLE my now well beloved Wife do hereby for a certain parcell of land lying in the FORREST of PISCATACON CREEK transferred over unto me by way of Exchange as will appear by Deed of Sale from under the hand & seale of JNO: GAINES of the same County, Planter, as also for divers other good causes relinquish assigne & make over all my right & interest in ye within recited premisses of land transferred over unto me sd PETER TREBLE by THO: PETTIS of KING & QUEEN County as doth more at large appear, the within Deed of Sale together with ye Patent & all other papers unto the aforesd. JNO: GAINES his heirs & assignes for ever wch: I the sd PETER TREBLE do

hereby warrant from ye title or claim of me my heirs or assignes or any other persons under me unto ye aforesd. JNO. GAINES In Witness whereof wee the sd PETER & ELIZA: TREBLE have set our hands & fixed our seales this 16th day of Sept: 1700
Signed sealed & delivered in prsence of us

RICHD. JONES — PETER P TREBLE
WILLIAM DUNN — ELIZ: E TREBLE
JA: CLERKE

Acknowledged by PETER TREBLE & right of Dower relinquished by ELIZA: his Wife in Essex County Court ye 10th day of 8br: 1700 & truely recorded

p. 58 In Obedience to an Order of Essex County Court bearing date ye 10th: day of 7ber: Ano: 1700, the Subscribers being lawfully sworne before Capt. RICHARD COVINGTON have appraised ye Estate of JNO: BILLINGTON lately deced to ye best of our knowledge ye 3d day of October 1700

To a parcell of pott iron qt. 162 lbs. at 2d p; To 27 lbs. of Brass at 7d p:, To 56 lbs. pewter at 9d p; 2 spitts, 2 old frying pans & flesh forke, two earthen plates, a parcell of old iron, 1 old chest, 1 old barrell, 2 old pailes, 2 pair of old fire tongs, pair pot racks, 1 brass candlestick, 4 pair sheets, 1 feather bed bolster blanket & rugg, 1 feather bed bolster rugg & blanket & pillow curtains as stands, 1 sadle, 1 chest drawers, 2 tables & forme; 2 pistols & holsters & Carbine, 1 warming pann, to Bellows, goose & sheers, 6 old chairs, 2 feather beds & furniture, 1 flocke bed & furniture, dimity, 4 yds Pennyston, Cotton, Druggt. & 1 shute Druggt. & old Coat, canvas, 1 deer skin, 1 looking glass, 2 old boxes & old trunks, 1 Negroe girl, 1 Servt. man 6 years to serve, 1 servt. man 5 years to serve, 1 servt. man 2 years to serve, 8 cows & 2 calves, 3 horses, 2 Steere 4 years old, 3 younger, 1 gray gelding 7 years old, 1 old Mare, 1 cross cut saw file & rest, 1 broad ax & hand saw, 1 set wedges, some old spoons, a parcell of old Bookes, 2 old Skilletts, 1 brass mortar & pestle, 1 grnstone:, 1 horse Total 140...3...2

WM. COVINGTON, — MARY HH BILLINGTON her mark
JERE: I SHEPARD
THOMAS T WADKINS

The above appraisers were sworn before me ye 2d day of 8:br 1700
p RICH: COVINGTON

Presented by MARY BILLINGTON, Admrx. of JNO: BILLINGTON deced upon Oath at a Court held for Essex County ye 10th day of October 1700 & truely recorded
Test FRANCIS MERIWETHER, Cl Cur

pp. 58-59 THIS INDENTURE made the 8th day of October in ye year of our Lord One thousand seven hundred. Now Know yee that JAMES JONES of Sittinburn Parish in ye County of Essex, Planter, & KATHERINE my Wife for the sum of Two thousand Five hundred pds. of tobo: & caske in hand paid or secured to be paid have sold unto the sd CHARLES BROWNE his heirs, Exers. Admrs. & assignes forever my part of a Devident of land left to my Wife, KATHERINE, by her Father, ROBT. ARMSTRONG, it being part of Four hundred acres of land Patented for my Father, ARMSTRONG, ye twenty six of 8:ber 1666 then assigned to NICHOLAS CATLETT ye 20th Febry: One Thousand six hundred & seventy two & then the sd NICHO: CATLETT by a Power of Attorney to Mr. EDMD. COOKE bearing date ye 17th of June 1672; acknowledged ye said land unto the aforesd. ARMSTRONG his heirs Exrs. Admrs. & assignes, the sd land being in RAPPA: County binding upon ye North side of PISCATTAWY CREEK as by Patent will more at large appear together with all edifices woods profits appurtenances wt:soever To have & to hold to him the sd CHARLES BROWNE his heirs or assignes forever & ye sd JAMES JONES and KATHERINE my Wife for ourselves our heirs warrant to defend ye sd land from the claime of any manner of persons and that the sd CHARLES BROWNE his heirs & assignes shall forever hereafter hold the sd tract of land paying yearly for Rent due for ye same to our Sovereigne Lord ye King his heirs & successors as Cheif Lord of the fees. In Witness whereof we have hereunto set our hands and fixed our seales this 10th day of October 1700

Signed sealed & delivered in the pr:sents of us

ROBERT KAY, JAMES JONES

JOHN ELLITT KATHERINE /K JONES

Acknowledged in Essex County Court ye 10th day of October 1700 by JAMES JONES & KATH: his Wife (ye sd KATH: being examined did it freely without compulsion of her sd Husband) & truely recorded Test FRANCIS MERIWETHER, Cl Cur

p. 59 Capt. GREGSON please to appear for me the next Court held for Essex County to prosecute an accon agt: DOCTR. ALEXANDER SPENCE and for you so doing you will much oblige your humble Servt.

ELIZABETH KING

Aprill ye 2d: 1700 truely recorded Test FRANCIS MERIWETHER, Cl Cur

p. 59 THIS INDENTURE made the 10th day of October Ano: Dom: 1700 Between Capt. JNO. CATLETT & Mr. DANL. DOBYNS, Justices of ye Peace of Essex County on ye behalfe of THO: EVANS, Orphan of JNO. EVANS, late of the sd County of Essex deced, of ye one part & THOMAS HUCKLESCOTT of the sd County of the other part Witnesseth that ye sd Capt. JNO. CATLETT & Mr. DANL. DOBYNS Gent. by & with ye consent & approbation of ye Worpll. Court of Essex County as by an Order dated ye 10th of 7:ber 1700 doth appear do by these presents put & bind the sd THO: EVANS an Apprentice with the sd THOMAS HUCKLESCOTT to serve the sd THO: HUCKLESCOTT & MARY his Wife from ye day of the date of ye above recited order untill he shall attaine unto ye age of twenty years dureing all wch: time the said THOMAS EVANS shall the sd THO: HUCKLESCOTT & MARY his Wife well & fully serve and toward them hon.stly & obediently behave himselfe & orderly & honestly toward all the rest of his family and the sd THO: HUCKLESCOTT for his aprt promiseth during the time untill the sd THO: EVANS cometh to ye age of twenty years to find unto the sd THO: EVANS meat drink washing linen woollen hose shoes & other things needfull & meet for an Apprentice & teach or cause him to be taught to read, wright & cast accots. as pr Ordr:, he being Twelve years old on ye Sixth day of Janry. next. In Witness whereof the parties have set their hands & seales

Signed sealed & delivered in presence of us

FRANCIS MERIWETHER, THOMAS HUCKLESCOTT

THO: GREGSON

Truely recorded according to Ordr: of Essex County Court ye 10h day of 8:br 1700

p. 59 TO ALL CHRISTIAN PEOPLE to whome these presents shall come greeting in our Lord God everlasting. Now Know ye that I ELIZ: GREGORY of Essex County for divers good causes & consideracons me hereunto moveing but more especially for ye tender love & affection wch: I have & do bear unto my Grand Child, BENJA:, ye Son of JNO. AIRES, do freely & absolutely give unto the aforesd. BENJA: AIRES of the aforesd. County one Cow & Calfe as also one young Mare going on three years old with all their encrease unto ye sd BENJA: AIRES

SAMLL. COATES ELIZABETH T GREGORY

Acknowledged in Essex County Court ye 10th day of October 1700 & truely recorded

p. 59 In Obedience to an Order of Court bearing date ye 12th of Aprill 1700, wee ye Subscribers have appraised ye Estate attacht. of JNO: TWIGGER for a debt of EDWD. DANIELLs this 20th of May 1700

May ye 12th 1700 Cor me Just: JOHN CATLETT

To 1 Cow & calfe, 1 cow bugg with Calfe, 2 barren cowes, 3 yearling calfes Total 2600 JOHN HAWKINS
DAVID WILSON
SAML. HENSHAW

Truely recorded Test FRANCIS MERIWETHER, Cl Cur

pp. 59-60 The Inventory & Appraismt. of the goods & chattells right & credits of JNO. SORRELL late of the County of Essex, deced.

Imprs. a feather bed & furniture curtains valence & bedstead; a table two forms & a carpet; a saddle; pistolls, holsters & furniture; an old bridle & saddle & saddel cloth; a parcell of Bookes; a weight seales two locks & a pl: of small stilliards; a doz. of napkins & two table cloathes, 5 sheets, two old truncks, a chest, a box & a cradle; a spining wheel & parcell of lumber; a gunn; a feather bed furniture curtains & valence & bed stead; a feather bed & furniture & bed stead; two chests & what is in them; a parcell of Nales & a box, a parcell of tooles & a box, a silver dram cup; a dozen of plates; 4 dozen of spoons & a salt; a parcell of pewter; a parcell of lumber; a parcell of tooles; an old Clapboard Chest; 2 pots skillet driping pan pott racks pestle &c., a parcell of old hoes, 6 sheep, a table, a bed, a horse, a man Servant, a Bill of DAVID JENKINS, a Bill of JNO. BUTLERs assigned; 2 cows & 2 calves, 4 yearlings, a steer of two years old, a heifer two years old, 3 steers each 4 years old, 5 cows, a bull, a colt, an old Cart & wheels, an old copper kettle, 3 grinstones Total 06510

RICHD. GOODE
JOHN M MILLS
DAVID D JENKINS

Yee 18th 7:br 1700. Sworne before me ROBT. BROOKE Total Tobo: 18979

Presented by DORCAS SORRELL, Exex. of JNO: SORRELL deced, upon Oath at a Court held for Essex County ye 11th of October 1700 & truely recorded Test FRANCIS MERIWETHER

P. 60 In Obedience of an Order of Essex County Court baring date the 10th day of Aprill 1700 & being sworne before Mr. DANL. DOBINS have appraised the Estate of RICHD. CARTER deced as was presented to our vewe as folloeth:

1 ollde flocke bead & farniture & an ollde bedstead, 1 ollde feather bed & farniture; a Man Servant haveing about two years to serve, 1 olde flocke bed, 2 olde trayes & 2 chares & 1 old bed stead; 3 earthen panes, 2 old earthen potes, 3 iarien potes & pesell, 1 fring pan, 3 chares, 1 old poudering tube & olde Skillet, 2 olde Cheestes, 3 steares, 1 cow & calfe, boles & two two yeare oyldes, 4 cowes & fore callfes, 1 barrand cow 7202

Presented by JNO: BROOKS (Admr. debonis non, Admr. of RICH: CARTER deced) upon Oath at a Court held for Essex County ye 11th day of October 1700 Test FRANCIS MERIWETHER, Cl Cur

THOMAS GREENE
HENRY hw WOODNUT
ANDREW A DUDING
THOMAS T COGING

P. 60 Mr. GEORGE LOYD. I request you to answer for me in the Suit of Mr. SORELL and for your so doing this shall be your warrant. Given undr: my hand this 10th 8:br 1700. Mr. MERIWETHER has ye Bill wch: please to demand if occasion

Yours D. G.

Truely recorded Test FRANCIS MERIWETHER, Cl Cur

pp. 60- 61 In Obedience to an Ordr: of Essex County Court to us directed ye Subscribers being sworn by HENRY GOARE, Sub Sher: have apprased such part of ye Estate of THO: COVINGTON deced as was p:sented to us by MARY COVINGTON, Administrx. of ye deced to which we have appraised the goods as followeth vizt.

(A partial list): Cows -10, 1 three year old bull, 2 steares, 2 horses, 31 lbs. of old puter, 26 pds. of new puter, 1 brass citell, 1 puter tankitt, tongs, spitt, chafing dish, frin: pans, parcell of old barrels &1 rimlett; 4 shickolls, 2 old trases, parcell of earthen ware; 1 old trunk, hose, axe, 2 old pailes, 1 flock bedd and two ruggs and one blankitt & bedstead, parcell of Servants beds, 3 wedges, whipsaw & an old hand saw, 1 drughett suite and a pr. of worsit stockings, 1 suit of cloths, 2 old coates, an old corrolina hatt; an old coate, 5 hatts, worsit stockins, girles stockins, mens ditto, womens ditto, 5 percers, 2 pr. mens shoes, 3 pr. girls ditto, 2 Lawes, chissells and an Agur:, hand vice, 2 pad locks, 1 cooper howell, 1 saddle, blankett, thred, 1 trunck, 9 doz: of Butt: thread, silke, 2 gro: of best butt: 1 pr. of gloves, 1 gro: more, nar: blew tape, 1 pr: of spurrs, 1/2 doz: of knives, 2 prs. of sissers, 1 pr. of shooes, 4 yds. of red stript crape, 6 yds. of anterregigne, blue lin: ticking printed ticking, 5 fine hatts, 1 chest, a sadle and furniture, 2 pr. of Ichabed bootes, a Buck Skin, eight cheires, fower matted cheires, a case and eight bottles, table, cabinetts, 3 Bibles, (many yards & ells of lining, ticking, serve, camlett, callimined, ozenbridge, canvas, cotton, broad cloath, kersey) sheets, ruggs, pillow bears, ruggs, 3 Ivory combs & two horne combs, a white dimeothy Jacquett, five shifts, a man servant named EDWARD SALMON 3 years to serve next Christmas, a boy named JOHN AKIN to serve ten yeares and a hafle, To an old Negroe named Boson, a Guiny, a Silver Cup, a Dram Cup

RICHARD R TYLER
JONATHAN FISHER
FRANCIS BROWNE
HENRY h WOODNOT

Since come to hand Trufle frame, bedstead, 1 pr. of Silver Shoo buckles MARY X COVINGTON
181=01=05 3/4

Sworne to in Essex County Court the 11th day of Febry: 1700 by MARY COVINGTON, Admrx. of THOMAS COVINGTON deced, & truely recorded Test FRANCIS MERIWETHER Cl

pp. 61- 62 THIS INDENTURE made this twenty sixt day of November in ye yeare of or: Lord One thousand seven hundred and in the Twelft yeare of the reigne of or: Dread Sovereigne William the third by the grace of God King of Greate Brittain, France and Ireland &c. Betweene Mr. JOHN PRICE of Farnam Parish in Essex County and Collony of Virginia, Chyrurgion, and HANNAH his Wife on the one part and RICHARD TAYLER of the aforesd Pish. & County, Planter, on the other part Witnesseth that the said JOHN PRICE and HANNAH his Wife for diverse good considerations but more especially for the sum of fower thousand pounds of sweete scented tobo: and cask to them in hand paid or secured to be paid hath granted for themselves their heires and administrators for and dureing the naturall life of HANNAH, his now Wife, a parcell of land and Plantation being in the aforesaid Pish. of Farnam and County of Essex being formerly the Plantation of ROBERT TAYLER since deceased and bequeathed in his last Will and Testament unto the aforesaid HANNAH, now the Wife of JOHN PRICE, dureing her naturall life conteyning by estimation Three hundred acres of land (more or less) together with all wayes waters and appurtenances to the same belonging and all the rights the said JOHN PRICE and HANNAH his Wife now hath unto the said p:misses To have & to hold unto he said RICHARD TAYLER his heires and assignes for and dureing the naturall life of the afore mentioned HANNAH now Wife to the aforesaid JOHN PRICE And that he will warrant & defend the said RICHARD TAYLER his heirs and assignes in the quiett and peaceable possession of the above bargained land against all persons whatseover that shall lay any claim In Witness whereof the said JOHN PRICE & HANNAH

his now Wife hath sett their hands and seales
Signed sealed & delivered in the pr:sence of

JONATHAN FISHER, JOHN PRICE
JOHN HARPER HANNAH H PRICE
THOMAS HARPER

Acknowledged by JNO: PRICE & HANNAH his Wife in Essex County Court the 10th day of xber 1700 (ye sd HANNAH being examined according to Law own'd that he Deed is freely & voluntarily without compultion of her Husband) & truely recorded Test FRANCIS MERIWETHER, Cl Cur

p. THIS INDENTURE made this 10th day of xbr: in the yeare of or: Lord God 1700 and
62 in the Twelfth yeare of the Reigne of or: Dread Sovereigne William the third &c.
Betweene JOHN HARPER of Farnham Parish in the County of Essex & Colony of Virga:, Planter, and LIDIA his Wife of the one part and JOHN PRICE of the aforesaid Parish & County, Chyrurgion, on the other part Witnesseth that the said JOHN HARPER and LIDIA his Wife for the sume of Two thousand pounds of sweet scented tobacco & caske to them in hand paid hath granted the said JOHN PRICE his heires Exers. & Administrs. a parcell of land lying and being in the aforesaid Parish & County upon the branches of PISCADDAWAY bounded as followeth beginning at the mouth of a branch caled & knowne by the name of the MIRIE BRANCH and runing up the said Branch to a line of COLD HILLS & along the said line to a corner red Oake by JOHN PRICE & along his line to a Great Swamp & down the said Swamp to the beginning as the beginning is a white Oake conteyning by estimacon a hundred acres of land together with all wayes waters profits to the same belonging and all the right which he the said JOHN HARPER now hath; To have & to hold all the said land with the appurtenances unto the said JOHN PRICE his heires & assignes & that the same shall be and remaine unto him for ever free & cleare and sufficiently kept harmless from all former incumbrances whatsoever And Lastly that he the said JOHN HARPER and LIDIA his Wife by herselfe or Lawfull Attorney shall make due acknowledgmt. of these pr:sents and her right of Dower in open Court the next Court to be held for Essex County when thereunto required In Witness whereof the said JOHN HARPER and LIDIA his Wife hath sett their hands and seales in the presence of HEN: GOARE, JNO: HARPER
SAM: COATES

Acknowledged in Essex County Court the 10th day of December 1700 and truely recorded

pp. THIS INDENTURE made the 5 day of October in the yeare of or: Lord God One
62- thousand six hundred ninety and nine Betweene GILLES CURTIS of the County of
63 MIDDX., Planter, of the one party, WILLIAM HUDSON of the County of Essex, Planter, of the other party Witnesseth that the sd GILES CURTIS for a valuable sume to be paid on demand hath granted unto the said WILLIAM HUDSON his heires and assignes Two hundred acres of land being part of a parcell of land formerly Mr. NICHOLAS COCKE bounded on the land of Mr. COCKE and on the land of HENRY WOODNOTT and runing alonge the DRAGON SWAMP side To have and to hold all the hereby sould premisses with their appurtenances to him the said WILLIAM HUDSON his heires and assignes for ever together with all woods waters and all other rights to the same belonging & the said WILLIAM HUDSON his heires paying the Kings Quit Rents therefore due and acostomed and the said GILES CURTIS doth for himselfe his heires promise that the sd p:misses with their app:tenances cleare from all other sales and incumbrances and that he the said WILLIAM HUDSON shall quietly and for ever enjoy all the said hereby sould pr:misses and the rights belonging without the lawfull trouble or deniall

of him his heires or any clayming under him. In Witness whereof the said GILES CURTIS hath hereunto sett my hand and seale

Signed sealed & delivered in pr:sence of

CHRISTOPHER BERNARD, GILES 9 CURTIS

RICE CURTIS

RICE CURTIS by virtue of a Power of Attorney from GILES CURTIS acknowledged this Deed of Sale in Essex County Court ye 10th day of November 1699 and the same is duely recorded

KNOW ALL MEN that WM. HUDSON of Essex County my heirs doe bargaine sell & make over unto GILES CURTIS of MIDLESEX County his heires &c. all that p:cell of land within mentioned with warranty from any claimes from any persons that may lay any claime to any pte: of the said land under me and acknowledge the same in Court held for the County of Essex wth: my Wife then and there to acknowledge her right of Dower in the within mentioned land In Witness whereof I hereunto sett my hand and seale this 23d day of November 1700

Signed sealed in pr:sence of

THOMAS MERIWETHER, WILLIAM W HUDSON

RICE CURTIS

Acknowledged in Essex County Court the 11th day of December 1700 & truely recorded

p. 63 Wee the Subscribers in Obedance of & Order of Essex County Corte. baring date the 11 day of October 1700 being sominiesed by the Sheriffe of the said County & swarane by Capt. RICHARD COVINGTON to vewe & reporte the damages don by Mr. ELIZABETH BRADLEY upon the land of WILLIAM COLEs doe reporte ass followeth that Mrs. ELIZABETH BRADLEY hath committed damages to the valley of tow pounds five shillings sterling money upon the sd COLE land. Given under our hands and seales this 28 day of October 1700

JONATHAN FISHER	EDMUND ROBARTS
JA: FULLERTON	WILLIAM C COX
WILLIAM RA AKUE	RICHARD JONES
THO: EVETT	JOHN HARPER
JOHN HAILES	WILLIAM DUN
ROBT: M RICHARDSON	

Truely recorded Test FRANCIS MERIWETHER, Cl Cur

p. 63 KNOW ALL MEN by these pr:sents that I ROBERT HALSEY of Farnham Parish in the County of Essex, Taner, doe by these pr:sents give unto THOMAS JOHNSON of the said County, Planter, a grand and firme Bill of Sayle of a tract of One hundred acres of land lying neer the head of PISCADWAY CREEKE which formerly did belong to a Track of Twelve hundred acres of land belonging to SAMUELL PERRY and then from the said PERRY made over to ROBERT YOUNG and sould by the aforesaid ROBERT YOUNG to THOMAS COOPER and sould from the said COOPER to RICHARD HACKINS and the said RD. HACKINS dying fell to his Son, JOHN HACKINS, & the said JNO. HACKINS dying without heire was escheated by ROBERT HALSEY which I doe hereby acknowledge the same in Essex Court at any time when required. I doe oblige myselfe my heires to warrant him and his heires against all manner of persons as my p:tent any right or title to the said land and with a good assurance from me and my heires forever. In Witness whereof I have hereunto putt my hand this Fifteenth day of October One thousand seaven hundred

Being pr:sent as witness
AUG: MEKAN, ROBT. HALSEY
BEN: SMITH
PETER PL MARKE
Acknowledged in Essex County Court ye 11th day of 9:ber 1700 & truely recorded

p. Essex County sc. The Deposicon of JAMES BOUGHAN aged 45 yeares or there-
63 abouts saith that about 13: or 14: years ago or thereabouts one RICHARD BOND
came out of MARYLAND & his Wife and brought with them one little girl as I doe believe might be about eight or nine yeares old and did severall times heare the said BONDs Wife say that that girl was her Daughter that she had by a former Husband & that her name was ELIZ: MUFFIT & that the said girl is now marryed to HENRY JOHNSON in this County & fuder saith not

JA: BOUGHAN

Xber: ye 9th day 1700. The Deposicon within written was proved by the within named JAMES BOUGHAN in Essex County Court the 11th day of Xbr: 1700 and is truely recorded according to an Order of the said Court Test FRANCIS MERIWETHER Cl Cur

p. Essex County ss. the Deposicon of JNO. WEBSTER aged 50 yeares or thereabouts
63 saith that about 14: or 15: yeares agoe Mr. RICHARD BOND & his two Sons arrived
att my House telling me they came from MARYLAND at their request I gave them Entertainment & some time after he sent for his Wife & Daughter & accordingly they came & I heard the said BONDs Wife say very often that that was her Daughter which she had by a former Husband whose name was MUFIT & that her name was ELIZ: MUFITT & I heard her Father in Law, Mr. RICHARD BOND & his two Sons say the very same & this ELIZ: whose sirname was formerly MUFITT is now the Wife of HENRY JOHNSON & I heard the said BOND & his Wife say that when they in in MARYLAND they lived upon an ISLELAND in PUTTOWCENT RIVER and further saith not

JNO. WEBSTER

The Depocion within written was proved by the within named JOHN WEBSTER in Essex County Court the 11th day of Xbr: 1700 & is truely recorded according to an Ordr: of the Court

p. KNOW ALL MEN by these pr:sents that I EDWARD DONOLIN doe impower SALVA-
63 TOR MUSCOE to receive for me and to my use all debts due to me in this County
and if any person doe deny the paymt. of any of the debts unto the said SALVATOR MUSCOEs hands then I doe hereby impower my said loveing Friend, SALVATOR MUSCOE, to prosecute the person or persons soe denying by an lawfull meanes whatsover, and whatsoever my said Attorney shall act or doe in the premisses I doe confirm to be as valid in the Law as if I my selfe were there pr:sent as Witness my hand and seale this 10th day of Xbr: 1700
Signed sealed in the pr:sence of us
ROBT. COLEMAN, EDWARD DONOLAIN
FRAN: MOORE
Prov'd in Essex County Court ye 11th Xbr: 1700 by the oathes of ye Witnesses & truely recorded

p. Essex ss. Whereas it has been made appeare to me by Mr. ROBERT HALSEY that
63 ROGER GRAY standeth indebted to hin by Accots. the sum of Two hundred & fifty
pounds of tobacco & is suspected imediately to absent the County whereby the

ordinary way of proceeding att Law cannot be had agt. him, These are therefore in his Majties. name to will and impower you to seize soe much of the Estate of ye said ROGER GRAY where it may be found in this County as will satisfie the said Debt with costs and the same to secure till the next Court held for the County & then and there to returne this Precept and make report of yor: proceeding thereon hereof faile not Given under my hand this 31th of Janry: 1699

To RICH: JONES, Constbl. THO: EDMONDSON

To Ex: & Ret. Febr: ye 8th day 1700 Then Execute the within Preceipt in the hands of Mr. SAMUEL PAREY the day and yeare as abovesd.

RICHARD JONES

Truely recorded Test FRANCIS MERIWETHER, Cl Cur

p. 64 IN THE NAME OF GOD, Amen. I THO: WHEELER in the Parish of South Farnham in ye County of Essex being in perfect sence and memory thanks be unto God for itt doe make this my last Will and Testament this 30th day of August 1698

First, I give and bequeath my Soule unto Almighty God hoping for pardon of all my sins through the meritts of my blessed Lord and Saviour Jesus Christ my body I give unto the Earth to be descently and Christianly intered as my Execterive hereafter named shall think fitt and for my worldly estate which the Lord lent me after my just debts and funerall charges be sattisfyed I give in manner following:

Imprs. I give unto my Daughter, MARY, two Ewe lambes to be paid her when she comes to fifteen yeares of age and all their increase forever ye sayd Lambes to be 6 moneths ould

I give unto my Daughter, ELIZABETH, two Ewe lambes to be paid her when she comes to Fifteen yeares of age and all their increase forever ye sayd lambes to be 6 moneth ould

I give unto my Daughter, ANN, two Ew lambes and one cow Calfe ye sayd Calfe & lambes to be seven moneths ould apeice and all their increase forever to be paid her att Fifteen yeares of age

I give unto my Son, THOMAS, two cow calves and two Ews of one yeare ould to be paid him when he comes to Fifteen yeares ould to him and heres withall their increase for ever

I give unto my Son, ROBERT, and to my Son, RICHARD, and to my Son, JOHN, each of them one Cow Calfe and two Ew lambes of seven moneths ould a peece with all their increase forever to be paid them as they come to the age of Fifteene years ould

All the rest of my Estate I give unto my loving Wife, ELIZABETH WHEELER, and I doe appoint & ordaine my loving Wife my whole and sole Execectorize of this my last Will and Testament and this to disannull all former Wills Gifts or Deeds whatsoever as Wittnesseth my hand and seale the day and year first above written

Signed sealed and delivered in the pr:sents of us

MARY MG GORBELL THO: WHEELER

THOMAS GORBELL

Prov'd by the Oathes of the Witnesses hereto in Essex County Court the 30th day of Xber: 1700 & truely recorded Test FRANCIS MERIWETHER, Cl Cur

KNOW ALL MEN that wee ELIZABETH WHEELER, THO: EDMONDSON & JAMES BOUGHAN of the County of Essex are firmely bound unto JOHN CATLETT Gent., President of the said County Court, in the sume of One hundred pounds Sterl. we bind ourselves this 30th day of Xber: 1700

The Condicon of this obligation is that if ELIZ: WHEELER who att a Court held for Essex County the day & yeare abovesd. obteyned a Probate of the last Will of THOMAS WHEELER deced shall att all times herefter fullfill the said Will and fully pay & satisfie all such

Legatees as therein are expressed and performe all ye Law enjoynes in such cases, the above obligation to be void otherwise to stand in full force
Signed sealed and delivered in presence of us

HEN: GOARE, ELIZABETH E WHEELER
THO: HUCKLESCOTT THO: EDMONDSON
JAMES BOUGHAN

Truely recorded Test FRANCIS MERIWETHER, Cl Cur

p. 64 IN THE NAME OF GOD Amen. this 11th day of Decembr: in ye yeare of or: Lord God 1700 I WILLIAM LEAKE of Farnham Parish in the County of Essex, Miller, being weake in body and of sound & perfect sence & memory and knowing the uncertainty of this life on Earth and being desireous to settle my worldly Estate which God of his greate Mercy hath endowed me with in order do make and ordaine this my last Will and Testament in manner and forme following:

Imps. I recommend my Soule into the hands of God Almighty my Creator assuredly believing that I shall receive full pardon & remission of all my sins and be save & precious Death of my blessed Saviour & redeemer Jesus Christ and my body to ye Earth from whence it was taken to be buryed in decent and Christian like manner as my Executrix hereafter named shall see convenient, Also I revoke and make void all former Wills by me made & declare & appoint this my Last Will and Testament

Item I will that all those debts and duties that in Right or conscence I doe lawfully owe or stand indebted to any manner of person whatsoever shall be well & truely pd. in some lawfull time after my decease by my Executrix.

Item I give unto my Godson, WILLIAM NEALE, one Cow & Calfe to be paid him when he comes of age to him and his heires forever

Item I give unto WILLIAM HARPER, the Son of JNO: HARPER, one Cow & Calfe the same to be paid him when he comes of age to him and his heires for ever

Lastly, I give & bequeath unto my now well beloved Wife, MARY LEAKE, my House and Planation with all the rest of my lands in Virginia or elsewhere whatsoever and also all the rest of my Estate both reall & personall whatever or wherever with all Bills bonds Dues or demands whatsoever that is any wayes owing or due to me the same I give unto her and her heires for ever whom I make & appoint my whole & sole Executrix of this my last Will & Testament In Witness whereof I the sd WM. LEAKE have hereunto set my hand and fixed my seale this day yeare first above written

WILLM. AA ACRES WILLM. W LEAKE
CHARLES CB BEGERLEY
JA: CLERKE

Prov'd by the Oathes of the Witnesses thereto in Essex County Court ye 30th day of Xber: 1700 & truely recorded Test FRANCIS MERIWETHER, Cl Cur

KNOW ALL MEN by these pr:sents that wee MARY LEAKE, JAMES BOUGHAN & JNO: HARPER of the County of Essex are firmely bound unto JNO: CATLETT Gent. President of the said County Court in ye sum of Two hundred pds. Sterl. we bind ourselves Witness or: hands and seales this 30th day of Xber: 1700

The Condition of this Obligation is such that if the above bound MARY LEAKE who att a Court held for Essex County the day and yeare abovesaid obteyned a Probate of the last Will of WM: LEAKE deceased shall and doe at all times hereafter performe ye said Will fully pay and satisfie all such Legatees as therein are expressed and doe performe all ye Law enjoines in such cases, Then he above obligation to be void otherwise to remaine in full force

HEN: GOAR
THO: HUCKLESCOTT

MARY W LEAKE
JAMES BOUGHAN
JOHN HARPER

Truely recorded Test FRANCIS MERIWETHER, Cl Cur

p. 65 KNOW ALL MEN by these pr:sents that wee SARAH DURHAM, JOHN MITCHELL & NICH: FOWLES of the County of Essex are firmely bound unto JOHN CATLETT Gent., President of the said County Court, in the sume of One hundred pounds sterling to the payment we bind ourselves this 30th day of Xbr: 1700

The Condition of this obligation is that if SARAH DURHAM, Admrx. of all & singular the goods chattles & creditts of WILLIAM DURHAM deced doe make a true inventory of all ye goods chattles & creditts of ye said deceds Estate which come to knowledge of her & exhibit ye same in next Court that shall be held for the abovesaid County of Essex and make Oath thereto & well and truely administer according to Law & further doe make a true & just Accot. of her administration when lawfully required & all the rest of th sd goods being first examined & allowed by the said Court shall deliver & pay unto such persons as ye sd Court appoints, that then this obligation to be void otherwise to remained in full force

Signed sealed and delivered in the pr:sence of
FRANCIS MERIWETHER,
JA: CLERKE

SARAH 3 DURHAM
JNO: N MITHCELL
NICH: f FOWLES

Truely recorded Test FRANCIS MERIWETHER, Cl Cur

p. 65 IN YE NAME OF GOD Amen. I RICHARD BUSH of ye County of Essex, Planter, being very sick but of parfect sence and memorey doe make & ordane my last Will and Testament in manner & forme following. Imprimis I give & bequeath my Sole to Allmighty God yt: gave it me & my body to ye yearth from whence it came hoping by the marsy of or: Loard & Savour Jesus Christ to receve a hapie and blessed Resurrection and as for my worleley estate which it has plesed God to possess me with after my just debts paid & satisfied I give and bequeath in manner & forme follering

Itim I give unto my beloved Wife, MARY BUSH, all my housell goods and catell hodghs and horses and cropp to hur and hur heirs forever onley my Wife paying all debts

Itim I give & bequith unto my Son, RICHARD BUSH, a Negro man called Jeffry to him & his heirs for ever

Itim I give & bequith unto my Son, JOHN BUSH, one cow called by the name of Starr to be delivered to him at my decease him and hur and hur increase to him and his heires for ever, And likewise my will and desire is that my Son, RICHARD BUSH, do pay unto JOHN BUSH, Five pounds starlen money of Ingland to be paid when he comes to he age of twenty one.

Lastley my will and desire is that my Wife, MARY BUSH, be hole Executrix of this my last Will & Testament. As Witness my hand & seale this 20th of October 1700

Signed sealed & delivered in pr:sents of us
JOHN WATERS,
NICKLES f FOWLES

RICHARD R BUSH

Prov'd by the oathes of the witnesses thereto in Essex County Court the 30th day of Xber: 1700 & truely recorded

KNOW ALL MEN by these pr:sents that wee MARY BUSH, WM. YOUNG and ROBERT WEBB of ye County of Essex are firmely bound unto JOHN CATLETT Gent., President of the said County Court, in the sume of One hundred pounds Sterl: to the payment we bind ourselves this 30th day of Xber: 1700

The Condicon of this obligation is such that if MARY BUSH who att a Court held for Essex County the day and yeare abovesd. obteyned a Probate of the last Will of RICHARD BUSH deced shall and do at all times hereafter fullfill ye sd Will and pay all such Legatees as are exprssed & performe all the Law enjoynes in such cases, That then this Obligcon to be void or else to remain in full force

Signed sealed & delivered in ye pr:sence of

HEN: GOARE, MARY O BUSH
THO: HUCKLESCOTT WILL: YOUNG
ROBT: R WEBB

Truely recorded Test FRANCIS MERIWETHER, Cl Cur

p. 65 March ye 9th 1699/1700. IN THE NAME OF GOD, Amen, I SUSANNA DAVIS being very sick & weake yet of perfect Minde & memory doe make & appoint this to be my last Will & Testament revoaking all other Will by me formerly maide eyther virball or to otherwise

Imprimis I give my sould unto the hands of Almighty God that gave itt my body to ye Grave desently to be intered wth such Christian buryall as time & place will afford. As to my worldly Welth I give in manner as followeth

Item I give unto my Sonne, JOB VIRGITT, twelve pence

My fether bed in the outer room with ye boulster rugg & one blankett I give to my Sonn, THOMAS MEADOWS, and the Table and three chaires in the outer room likewise to my Daughter, ELIZABETH SHIPP, I doe give my Warmg. pann my box & my trunk & all my wareing cloaths & all the rest of my Estate both goods and chattles within doores and without that apperteynth unto me I give to my Sonne, WILLIAM DAVIS, and Further my will is that my Sonne, THOMAS MEADOES be sole Executor of this my last Will and Testament as Witness my hand and seale this fifteenth of Febr: 1699

Teste WM. GANNOCKE SUSANNA DAVIS
WM: X SHORT

Prov'd by the oathes of ye Witnesses hereto in Essex County Court ye 30th: day of Xber: 1700 & truely recorded Test FRANCIS MERIWETHER, Cl Cur

KNOW ALL MEN that wee THO: MEADERS, THO: GREGSON & WM. GANNOCKE of the County of Essex are firmely bound unto JOHN CATLETT Gent., President of the said Court, in the sume of One hundred pounds Sterl. to the payment whereof we bind ourselves Witness our hands and seales this 30th day of Xbr: 1700

The Condicon of this obligation is that if THOMAS MEADERS who att a Court held for Essex County the day and yeare abovesaid obteyned a Probate of the last Will and Testament of SUSANNA DAVIS deceased shall att all times hereafter performe and fullfill the said Will, pay and satisfie all such Legatees as therein are expressed and doe performe whatsoever the Law enjoyns in such case then the above obligacon to be void otherwise to remaine in force

Signed sealed & delivered in ye presence of us

WILL: YOUNG THO: MEADERS T
FRANCIS MERIWETHER, THO: GREGSON
WM. GANNOCK

Truely recorded Test FRANCIS MERIWETHER, Cl Cur

p. 66 In Obedience to an Order of Essex Court beareing date the 30th: X:ber 1700 the Estate of WILLIAM DERHAM deced Inventoryed and appraised by us whose names are underwritten

Imprs. To 18 1/2 lbs. of pewter, parcell of tenn panns, 1 brass citell, halfe a dozen of spoones & candelstick, chambr: pott and bottle, parsell of yearthen ware, 1 bead and furniture, parcell of lining made up, 1 chest, 1 bed Tick and Bolster, 3 1/2 yds of Baggin linning, Coton, 9 ells of Streaten, Lockrum, Wol collored lining, Collard holland, Sharge, broad cloth, blew linning, 1 coate and vest, 1 coate, 2 caster hatts, 1 old Sword, parcell of iron, 2 gunns, 1 old Mare, 2 cowes and 2 yearlings, 70 lbs. of Pott iyron at 3 1/4 p pound, 1 Grindstone Total 50=07=03

The Apraisors sworne p me DANLL. DOBYNS

WILL: YOUNG
JOHN WATERS
THOMAS GREENE

Presented by SARAH DURHAM Admrx. of WM. DURHAM deced upon Oath to a Court held for Essex County ye 10th day of Febry: Anno Dom: 1700 & truely recorded

p. 66 IN THE NAME OF GOD Amen, I JNO. HINE of the County of Essex being sick & weake in body but of sound and perfect memory praised be God for the same, do make & ordaine this my last Will and Testament in manner and forme following, First I give my Soule to God that gave itt in ye hopes of a joyfull resurrection att the last Day and my body to the Earth to be decently interred after my decease & for my temporall Estate I give and bequeath as followeth:

Itm. I give and bequeath all my Estate to my Son, JOHN HYNE, to him and his heires for ever, Except Ten pounds Sterling which Capt. THO: GREGSON is indebted to me and out of which I stand indebted to him Six hundred and thirty pounds of tobo: which I desire my friend, ROBT. BROOKE, to satisfie and be accountable to my Son for the remainder

It is my will and desire that my Son, JOHN HINE, be and remain with my friend, ROBERT BROOKE, till he shall be the full age of one and twenty yeares

Itm. I make my Son, JOHN HINE, Sole Exerc. of this my last Will and Testament. In Testimony whereof I have hereunto putt my hand and Seale this 26th: day of X:ber 1700

Signed sealed & delivered in the pr:sence of

DAVID ↄ JENKINS,
FRANCIS ↑ JOHNSON

JNO: IH HYNE

The within written Will was proved by the oathes of DAVID JENKINS & FRA: JOHNSON in Essex County Court ye 10th day of Febry: Anno Dom: 1700 & truely recorded

KNOW ALL MEN by these pr:sents that we ROBT. BROOKE and THO: GREGSON of the County of Essex are firmely bound unto his Majties. Justices of the Peace for the said County in the sume of Twenty thousand pounds of good sound Merchantable tobo: and caske to the payment we bind ourselves this 10th day of Febry: 1700

The Condicon of the above obligacon is that if ROBT. BROOKE, Admr. with ye Will annexed of JNO: HINE deced dureing the Minority of JOHN HYNE, Exerc. of the said Will, doe make a perfect Inventory of all ye goods & creditts of the said deced & doe exhibit to the next Court held for the said County and make Oath thereto & truely administer on ye Estate according to Law and give a just accot. of his administracon when lawfully required, Then the above obligation to be void otherwise to remaine in full force

Signed sealed & delivered in pr:sence of us

FRANCIS MERIWETHER,
JOHN GOARE

RO: BROOKE
THO: GREGSON

Truely recorded Test FRANCIS MERIWETHER, Cl Cur

pp. 66-67 In Pursuance to an Ordr: of Essex County Court beareing date May ye 10th 1700 whereon it is ordered that wee the Subscribers doe Inventory & appraise the Estate of THOMAS HINDS deceased, that shall be pr:sented to us by HANNAH SPENCER, Ye Administr. of the deced THOMAS HINDS, as alsoe to take the Estate of

EBENEZER STANFEILD out of the said deceds Estate wee being sworne by Mr. DANIELL DOBBINS have accordingly taken out the said STANFEILDs Estate Inventoryed & appraised the sd deceds Estate as Witness our hands this fifth day of June 1700

Imprs. To 2 cowes sett as to of the Estate of EBENEZER STANFEILD, To Tobb: ye sume from the Estate due - 1700; To 1 horse also which is the said Estate; To 6 cowes, 6 yearlins, 3 steres, 3 heffers 2 years old, 1 heffer, 1 stere, 1 bull, 1 horse and 2 mares, 1 young mare filley, 1 Christian Servant, 1 old Negroe man; 1 Negroe woman, 1 Negroe girle, six deare skinks, Searge, Course lining, Canvas, narrow lining, Scoth Cloth, Virginia Cloath, Kersey, Course Kersey, Serge, broad blue, pennystone, haire cloth, demety, dyaper table lynning, course table lynning, sheeteing (Approx. 88 yards & 122 Ells various types of Cloth) Course thread, 2 Cobberd Cloaths & a slipe of Calico, parcell of Tape, parsell of Pepper, 65 lb. pewter, parsell of Tinn ware; 3 brass kettles, 1 box iron and heaters, 2 old frying panns, 2 iron potts and 1 iron kettell, 1 old gunn, a parsell of old Servants bedding, 1 table & case of table knives, 1 small Bible and 1 old Common Prayer Booke, 1 ovell table and 6 new leather chaires, 2 feather beds and furniture, 16 lbs. of feathers, 3 chests, 1 small trunck, 1 punch bole, 1 old side saddle and old Bridle, 13 lbs. unwarfed wooll, 1 old bos, 2 gall. runlett, 1 rule, p small stilliards, p:cell of carpenters old tooles, 2 pott racks, 1 spitt, 1 gridiron & flesh forke, 5 weeding hoes, 3 hilling howes & 1 axe, a parsell of old iron & other old things, 2 small looking glasses, 1 warming pan, two chesseles, 5 Sider caske, 2 gall. runlett, 2 meal tubbs, 2 meale sifter & 1 earthen pann, 1 butter tubb & spining wheele & 4 wedges, 3 old trayes, 6 round bottles 2 matted cheires, 2 pr. of shooes & two graters; 15 hundred 10d nayles, 3 horne Comb

ANDREW DUDDING his mark The sume totall 159=10=04
RICHARD BROOKE,
EDW. ADCOCKE

Presented by THO: SPENCER & HAN: his Wife, Exerx. of THO: HINES deced upon Oath to a Court held for Essex County ye 11th day of Febry: Anno Dom 1700 & truely recorded

p. 67 KNOW ALL MEN that wee RICHD. COVINGTON and THO: MERIWETHER Gent. of the County of Essex are firmely bound unto JOHN CATLETT Gent., President of the said County Court in the sume of One hundred pounds Sterl. to the paymt. we bind ourselves Witness or: hands & seales this 11th day of Febry: 1700

The Condicon of this obligation is that if the above bound RICHD. COVINGTON, Guardian of ELIZABETH COVINGTON, Orphan of THO: COVINGTON deced, his heires & Adminstrs: shall truely pay unto the said Orphan all such Estate as shall come to the hand of the sd RICHD: COVINGTON as soon as said Orphan shall attaine to lawfull age or when required by the Justices of the Essex County Court abovemenconed, as alsoe to save the said Justices from all trouble that may arise about the said Estate, Then the above obligation to be void, otherwise to remaine of full force

Signed sealed & delivd: in the prsence of us

FRANCIS MERIWETHER, RICHD. COVINGTON
THOMAS HUCKLESCOTT THOMAS MERIWETHER

Truely recorded Test FRANCIS MERIWETHER, Cl Cur

p. 67 KNOW ALL MEN that wee WILLIAM SOUTHERLAND of the County of KING & QUEEN & JNO. FISHER of the County of Essex are firmely bound unto JOHN CATLETT Gent. President of ye sd County Court, in ye sume of One hundred pounds Sterl. to ye true paymt. we bind ourselves this 11th day of Febry: 1700

The Condicon of this obligation is that if WILLIAM SOUTHERLAND, Guardian of ELIZ: COVINGTON, Orphan of THO: COVINGTON, his heires shall truely pay unto the said Orphan

all such Estate as shall come to the hands of ye sd WM: SOUTHERLAND as soon as ye sd Orphan shall attayne to lawfull age or when required by the Justices of the Court of Essex County as alsoe to save the said Justices from all trouble that shall arise about the said Estate, Then the above obligacon to be void otherwise to stand in full force
Signed sealed and delivered in the pr:sence of us

THOMAS SPENCER — WM. SOUTHERLAND
JOHN MAKEING — JONATHAN FISHER

Truely recorded Test FRANCIS MERIWETHER, Cl Cur

p. THIS INDENTURE made ye 22d. day of Janry: 1700 Betweene FRANCIS MERI-
68 WETHER of the County of Essex of the one part & RICHD. COVINGTON of the same County of the other prt Witnesseth that the said FRA: MERIWETHER for Two hundred & twenty five pounds of good & lawfull money of England truely paid hath sold unto the said RICHARD COVINGTON his heires and assignes forever that Plantacon whereon the said FRA: MERIWETHER now liveth & those severall tracts of land belonging to it (Except halfe a sole square of land includeing that place where the body of FRA: MERIWETHER, Son of the aforesd. FRA: MERIWETHER lyes inter'd) which the said FRA: MERIWETHER purchased of JAMES MERRIOTT by Deed dated ye 10th day of Febry: 1695 & acknowledged in the Court of the aforesd. County the same day, conteyning One hundred Eighty and eight acres & a halfe, one rood and eight poles, be the same more or less and all houses buildings orchards gardens waters woods & appurtenances to the same belonging & all the Estate right of him the said FRA: MERIWETHER to the same (Except as before Excepted) To have and to hold the said Plantation forever to the only proper use & behoofe of the said RICHD. COVINGTON his heirs & assignes, he paying the rents & performing ye services which shall hereafter become due unto or: Sovereign Lord ye King; And the said FRANCIS MERIWETHER for himselfe & his heirs will warrant & forever defend and said RICHD. COVINGTON shall henceforth peaceably hold and enjoy the said pr:misses without the trouble of the said FRANCIS MERIWETHER his heires or assignes In Witness whereof the said FRANCIS MERIWETHER hath set his hnd and seale
Signed sealed & delivered in pr:sence of

THO: LANE, — FRANCIS MERIWETHER
WM. X BULLOCK

FRA: MERIWETHER acknowledged this Deed of Sale to Capt. RICHD. COVINGTON at a Court held for Essex County ye 11th day of Febry: 1700 & Capt. WM. JONES by virtue of a Power of Attorney from MARY MERIWETHER, Wife of the said FRA: MERIWETHER, prov'd by ye oathes of Capt. WM. BIRD & THO: MERIWETHER relinquished her right of Dower to ye land therein menconed & ye same is truely recorded Test FRANCIS MERIWETHER Cl Cur

I the Subscriber doe hereby impower you Capt. WM. JONES to be my true and lawfull Attorney for me (as I am the lawfull & espoused Wife of Mr. FRANCIS MERIWETHER) to release in open Court held for Essex County all my right and interest of Dower that I have to one hundred eighty eight acres and hafle one rod & eight poles within the said bounds as is by my Husband, FRANCIS MERIWETHER, sold and conveyed to Capt. RICHD. COVINGTON by a Deed date ye 22d of Janry: 1700, and what my said Attorney shall act or doe I doe hereby confirme Witness my hand and seale this 11th day of Febry: 1700
Signed sealed and delivered in pr:sence of

WM. BIRD, — MARY MERIWETHER
THO: M MERIWETHER

Prov'd in Essex County Court ye 11th day of March 1700 by the Oaths of Capt. WM. BIRD & THO: MERIWETHER & truely recorded. Test FRANCIS MERIWETHER, Cl Cur

p. Decr: ye 29:th 1700. This is an Inventory of JOHN PEATLEs Estate
68 To six yards of Stuffe, To a hatt, To six yards of tinsy lase and to three yards of gause; To five shirts & a parcell of shirts and handkercheiffes, To flower ells and dowlas, To two yards and a halfe of Scotch cloth and to two muslin neck cloathes, To Five yards of Callaminco and five yeards of stuffe, a parcell of old Cloathes, To a coate and britches, a parcell of dimity and a parcell of Stuffe, a parcell of old Bookes, an old Trunck and some other small things, two old saddles and two old bridles, 2 paires of Stilliards and two paire of Cart hoocks and a hain, To a slate and two old hats and fouwer paire of shooes, To an old chest and little lumber, a little Bay horse, To tobb: received of his Debts., To one bagg, To one paire of brass Shoe Buckles, To one paire of Stockings, To one rimlett, To one Spurr, To three dozen and one Coate buttons, To 31 brest buttons, To eight Shillings Sterling money, To these articles to tobb: ordred. by the Vestry (0850)
As Witness or: hands Total 2610

EDMUND PAGETT
GEO: LOYDE
JOHN GRAVES

Pr:sented att a Court held for Essex County ye 11th day of Febry. Ano: Dom: 1700 by THO: MUNDAY, Admr. with the Will annexed, of JNO. PEATLE deced & truely recorded

pp. THIS INDENTURE made the tenth day of January in the yeare of or: Lord God
68- according to the Computation now used in the Church of England One thousand
69 and seaven hundred Between RANDALL BIRD of the Parish of Citenburne in the County of Essex, Sawyer, & ARABELLA his Wife, only Daughter & heire apparent of HENRY WHITE, late of the same Parish & County deced, of the one part and FRANCIS GOULDMAN of the said Parish and County Gent., of the other pte. Witnesseth that for the sume of Seaven thousand pounds of good merchantable tobacco unto the said RANDALL BIRD and ARABELLA his Wife in hand truely paid by the said FRANCIS GOULDMAN, they the said RANDALL BIRD and ARABELLA his wife have granted unto the said FRANCIS GOULDMAN his heires & assignes all that tract of land conteyning Three hundred acres be the same more or less being in the Pish. of Cittenburne & County of Essex aforesaid & bounded begining at a marked redd Oake menconed in JOHN BARROWEs Pattent to stand nigh the land of AUGUSTIN BRETHNBIRD runing thence West to a marked Gum, thence North to the CHURCH ROADE and along the said ROADE to a marked white Oake standing by a White Marsh, thence along the water course of the said Marsh to a Deep Branch & downe the Branch to the Maine Creeke, thence the severall courses of the Pattent to the place where it first began, with all & singular its rights & appurtenances together with all houses buildings barnes stalles orchards gardens trees which said Three hundred acres of land is part of a Pattent of Seaven hundred thirty & seaven acres & 145 pearches of land granted to JOHN BARROW by Pattent beareing date the 24th of March 1660 & all the Estate right as well in Equity as at Law of them the said RANDALL BIRD & ARABELLA his Wife or either of them to the same, To have and to hold unto the said FRANCIS GOULDMAN his heires and assignes forever paying the Rents & performeing the services which shall hereafter grow duw unto or: Sovereign Lord the King And the said RANDALL BIRD and ARABELLA his Wife for themselves their heirs the said land will warrant and forever defend and doe promise that he the said FRANCIS GOULDMAN his heires & assignes att all times forever hereafter peaceably enjoy the said land without any trouble of the said RANDALL BIRD & ARABELLA his Wife or any other persons whatsoever In Witness whereof the parties first above named their hands and seales have sett

Signed sealed & delivered in the pr:sence of

RO: BROOKE, RANDALL O BIRD
SAMLL. THACKER ARABELLA O BIRD
RO: PAYNE

Wee the within named RANDALL BIRD & ARABELLA my Wife do hereby acknowledge to have had & received the full sume of Seaven thousand pounds of tobacco by the Deed within written

Test RO: BROOKE, RANDALL O BIRD
SAMLL. THACKER ARABELLA O BIRD
RO: PAYNE

Acknowledged in Essex County Cort. ye 11th day of Febry: 1700 & truely recorded

RAND: BIRD and ARABELLA his Wife (ye said ARABELLA being first privately examined according to Law) acknowledged this Deed of Sale to Mr. FRA: GOULDMAN att a Court held for Essex County the 11th day of Febry: 1700 & its truely recorded

KNOW ALL MEN that wee RANDALL BIRD & ARABELLA my Wife, Only Daughter & heirs apparent of HENRY WHITE, late of the same Parish & County deced, are firmely bound unto FRANCIS GOULDMAN of said Parish & County, Gentl., in summe of Two hundred pounds of lawfull money of England to be paid we bind ourselves the Tenth day of January One thousand and seaven hundred

The Condicon of this obligacon is that if RANDALL BIRD & ARABELLA his Wife their heires truely perform all covenants on part of said RANDALL BIRD & ARABELLA his Wife ought to be kept in Indenture beareing equall date with these presents according to the purport of the same Indenture, Then this obligacon to be void or else to remaine in full force

Signed sealed & delivered in the pr:sence of us

RO: BROOKE, RANDALL O BIRD
SAMLL. THACKER ARABELLA O BIRD
RO: PAYNE

Acknowledged by RANDLL BIRD in Essex County Court 11th dayof Febry: 1700 and truely recorded

p. 70 The marke of HENRY SMITH is as followeth vizt., two crops & a slitt in each ear Truely recorded according to Ordr: of Essex County Court 11th of Febry: 1700

p. 70 KNOW ALL MEN by these pr:sents that wee THOMAS MERIWETHER, THO: GREGSON & FRANCIS MERIWETHER of the County of Essex are firmely bound unto JNO. CATLETT Gentl., President of the said County Court in the sume of Fifty pounds Sterl. to payment we bind ourselves this 11th day of Febry: 1700

The Condicon of this obligacon is that if THO: MERIWETHER, Admr. de bonis non Administratis of all the goods chattles & creditts of WM. SWETNAM deced doe make a perfect Inventory of all the goods chattles & credits of ye sd deced which have come to the hands of said Administrator & the same soe made doe exhibit to the next Court that shall be held for the County of Essex, & make Oath thereto and further doe make just Accot. when lawfully required & all the rest shall deliver & pay unto such p:sons as ye sd Court pursuant to Law shall appoint, Then this obligacon to be void otherwise to remaine in full force

Signed sealed and deld. in pr:sence of us

THOMAS HUCKLESCOTT, THOMAS MERIWETHER
JAMES EDMONDSON THO: GREGSON
FRANCIS MERIWETHER

Truely recorded Test FRANCIS MERIWETHER, Cl Cur

p. KNOW ALL MEN by these pr:sents that wee JNO: BUTTLER & JANE his Wife, THO:
70 GREGSON, & ROBT. PAYNE of the County of Essex are firmely bound unto JNO. CATLETT Gent., President of the said Court in the sume of Two hundred pounds Sterl. to the payment we bind ourselves this 11th day of Febry: 1700

The Condicon of this obligacon is that if the above bound JOHN BUTTLER & JANE his Wife, Administrators of all and singular the goods chattles and credits of ISAACK JACKSON deced doe make perfect Inventory of all the goods & creditts which come to the hands of them and the same doe exhibitt to the next Court that shall be held for the abovesd. County & make Oath thereto And further doe make a true & just accot. of their administracon when they shall be lawfully required & all ye remaining deliver to such persons as ye sd Court p:suant to Law shall appoint Then this obligacon to be void, otherwise to remain in full force and virtue

Signed sealed & delivered in the presence of us

THOMAS HUCKLESCOTT, JNO: BUTLER
SALVATORE MUSCOE JANE A BUTLER
THO: GREGSON
RO: PAYNE

Truely recorded Test FRANCIS MERIWETHER, Cl Cur

p. KNOW ALL MEN that wee ANDREW DUDDEN & EASTER my Wife of Essex County in
70 consideracon of Sixty pounds money of England sell unto DANLL. DOBYNS of ye sd County of Essex all our right of Two hundred acres of land which said land was made voer to me in time of my Widowhood from JOHN DICK of RAPPA. County on side of a Deed of Sale from JOHN & GEORGE KILLMAN unto ye sd JOHN DICKE bearingdate 3rd of May 1671 by an assignment from ye sd DICKE & acknowledged to me in ye County Court of RAPPA: bearing date ye 7th of May 1679; ye sd Two hundred acres of land scituated in ye County of Essex according to Survey of ye same by GEORGE MORRIS and bounded as followeth (vizt.) Beginning at a Spanish Oake on ye line of Capt. JOSIAS PICKES nigh ye GREENE BRANCH and runing over ye sd GREENE BRANCH West to a red Oake to a white Oake corner trees to ye first menconed Stake, To have and to hold unto ye said DANLL. DOBYNS his heires and assignes forever togeather with all privilidges all woods in as ample manner as it is expressed in Patent And we ye sd ANDREW DUDDEN & EASTER my Wife do promise to acknowledge our Deed in ye County Court of Essex at any time required In Witness whereof we hereunto set our hands and seales this 10th: day of March 1700

Signed sealed & delivered in pr:sence of us

JOHN CHENEY, ANDREW D DUDDIN
HENRY h WOODNUTT EASTER ED DUDDIN

Acknowledged in Essex County Cort. the 10th day of March 1700 by ye sd ANDREW DUDDIN & EASTER his Wife (ye said EASTER being examined according to Law own'd that the Deed is freely & voluntarily without compultion of her Husband) & truely recorded

KNOW ALL MEN by these pr:sents that wee ANDREW DUDDEN & EASTER his Wife of Essex County are firmely bound unto DANIELL DOBYNS of the aforesaid County in the sume of One hundred & twenty pounds Sterl., money of England, to confirm and acknowledge unto the aforesd. DANIELL DOBYNS in the said County Court aforesd. a Deed of Sale of Two hundred acres of land which wee the said ANDREW and EASTER DUDDIN have sold unto the aforesaid DANIELL DOBYNS his heires &c., And to keepe harmless the said DANLL. DOBYNS from the molestacon or claymes of any pesons whatsoever the which payment to be truely paid we bind ourselves as Witness or: hands and seales this 15th of Novembr: 1700.

The Condicon of the obligacon is if the above bounden ANDREW DUDDEN & EASTER his Wife their heires keepe harmless the abovesd DANLL. DOBYNS from the disturbance of any persons that shall lay any clayme to ye aforesaid Two hundred acres of land in the Deed of Sale above menconed bearing date with these presents Then this obligacon to be void or else to stand in full force as Witness or: hands and seales
Signed sealed & delivered in the pr:sence of us

JOHN CHENEY, — ANDREW AD DUDDIN
HENRY h WOODNUTT — EASTER ED DUDDIN

Acknowledged in Essex County Cort: the 10th day of March 1700 & truely recorded

p. 71 KNOW ALL MEN that wee JNO: CRASKE of the County of RICHMOND, THO: GREGSON & THOMAS MUNDAY of the County of Essex are firmely bound unto JNO. CATLETT, Gent., President of the said County Court in the summe of Three hundred pounds Sterl. to the payment we bind ourselves this 10th day of March 1700
The Condicon of this obligacon is that if JOHN CRASKE, Guardian of THO: BENDERY, Orphan of WM. BENDERY deced, his heires shall well and truely pay unto the said THO: BENDERY all such Estate as shall come unto the hands of the said JOHN CRASKE as soon as the said THO: BENDERY shall attaine to lawfull age or when required by the Justices of the Peace of Essex County as alsoe to keep harmless the said Justices from all damages that may arise, Then, the above obligacon to be void otherwise to remain in full power

JOHN CRASKE
THO: GREGSON
THO: Th MUNDAY

Acknowledgled in Essex County Cort: ye 10th day of March 1700 & truely recorded

pp. 71-72 KNOW ALL MEN by these pr:sents that we MARY COVINGTON & JAMES BOUGHAN of the County of Essex are firmely bound unto JNO: CATLETT Gent., President of the said County Court in sume of One hundred pounds Sterl: to the payment we bind ourselves Witness or: hands and seales this 11th day of Febry: 1770
The Condicon of this obligacon is that if the above bound MARY COVINGTON, Guardian of MARY COVINGTON, Orphan of THO: COVINGTON deced, her heires & Admrs. shall truely pay unto the said Orphan all such estate as shall come to the hands of the said MARY COVINGTON as soon as the said Orphan shall attaine to lawfull age or when required by the Justices of th Peace for Essex County Court & save & keepe harmless the said Justices from all trouble about the sd Estate Then the above obligacon to be void, otherwise to stand in full force
Signed sealed & delivered in pr:sence of us

FRANCIS MERIWETHER, — MARY X COVINGTON
THOMAS HUCKLESCOTT — JAMES BOUGHAN

Acknowledged in Essex County Cort: ye 10th day of March 1700 & truely recorded

www.ingramcontent.com/pod-product-compliance
Lightning Source LLC
Chambersburg PA
CBHW080337270326
41927CB00014B/3267